Advance Insights From The Field

Dynamic Relationships
Unleashing the Power of Appreciative Inquiry in Daily Living

"*Dynamic Relationships* signals the next generation of Appreciative Inquiry. It builds on the most powerful and mysterious of social constructionist principles, the relational nature of our selves. This is a powerful and comprehensive approach to connecting deeply and joyously with our most desired future."

> ~*Daniel K. Saint, Ph.D., Former Partner, Deloitte*

"To my knowledge this is the first book in the field of Appreciative Inquiry that combines theory and practice in such a fine way. It also makes provocative reading as the authors take a very clear stand in the dialogue whether AI will change your life or not: it will. Working through this book will increase your *awareness* of yourself, of your relations, and how to grow and enrich these relations. Taking this clear position not only makes this book refreshing as it fires up the dialogue around AI, but it also helps us readers—in a very practical way—to discover the next steps on the road that leads to the discovery of the positive core of ourselves and of others we are in relation with. Jackie Stavros and Cheri Torres have produced a challenging book that will inspire many of us to travel further in our search for the very best in our relationships!"

> ~*Joep de Jong, Director Learning Solutions Europe, BT, Amsterdam, Holland*

"Knowing both authors professionally, I am delighted they wrote this book. Jackie Stavros and Cheri Torres live the principles of *Dynamic Relationships* in their work and families. I am eager to get my hands on this book as a resource for clients and colleagues focused on positive change in health care."

> ~*Susan O. Wood, Principal, Corporation for Positive Change*

"I thoroughly enjoyed reading your manuscript. I got several good ideas relating to our graduate program and my own writing, not to mention some possibilities for changing my relationship with others. Thanks! This book does two things: first, by addressing life outside organizations, it helps make more people aware of the idea of living in the appreciative paradigm; and second, it helps make the idea real and useful to anyone who chooses to act on it. Jackie and Cheri have thus put before us a potentially life-changing tool that we can use to fashion our future in relationship with others beyond organizational life. The rest is up to us."

~*John M. Peters, Professor and Coordinator,*
Doctoral Program in Collaborative Learning,
University of Tennessee

"Cheri and Jackie invite us to be more mindful, self-aware, of the impact our daily conversations have on our personal and professional relationships. They also give us many experiential exercises to help us create conversations that support more positive and dynamic relationships. *Dynamic Relationships* is a practical contribution to the growing literature of Appreciative Inquiry."

~*Nancy Stetson, Ed.D., Center for Appreciative Inquiry*

"Stavros and Torres have made an exceptional contribution with this practical and thoughtful book. This piece takes Appreciative Inquiry beyond the organizational life into your life. It's an exciting and expansive relational paradigm to live each day."

~*Dr. Marge Schiller, President, The Positive Change Corps*

"A fantastic piece of work! The activities and exercises make this approach so real to live into. I especially found the briefcase exercise very helpful because it will get me home on time for dinner with my family."

~*David Gregorich, Manager of Electronics,*
Macomb Community College

"When my friend Jackie Stavros asked me to read and edit a book she had co-authored, *Dynamic Relationships: Unleashing the Power of Appreciative Inquiry in Daily Living*, I had no idea it would so reinforce an attribute much needed in my life at this time. In July of last year, I learned that I had Medullary Cancer of the Thyroid. This is a chronic and incurable affliction, which does not respond to Chemo Therapy or Radiation. Constant monitoring via blood tests, body scans, and surgical removal of any malignant lesions can control it. The "X" factor in controlling this disease is a *positive mental attitude.*

I defy anyone reading this book and performing the prescribed exercises to have anything but a positive outlook on life and the living relationships therein. As I write this piece, I am preparing for the fourth surgery in nine months. Now, thanks to *Dynamic Relationships*, I will not reflect upon how tired I am of being hospitalized, but rather upon how happy I will be when my surgeon tells me to get out of here and don't come back! Thanks Jackie and Cheri for sharing this bit of wisdom with me."

~Pat Riney, Sr., Poet and Author, Commerce, Michigan

"Making positive change happen in one's own life is the *real* challenge. The authors not only show us the path to a positive future, but also many practical activities to move us along that path. In particular, they have made the underlying principles of this change process 'come alive' as a result of their vivid and concrete examples."

~Paul Hilt, Principal, Hilt and Associates,
Berwyn, Pennsylvania

"*Dynamic Relationships* offers each of us a framework to understand, develop, and enhance the benefits and energy of strengths-based awareness. This heightened awareness provides insight into how we can 'live' our personal and professional relationships. Doing so leads to new, positive outcomes, and Principle of Awareness. Thank you Jackie and Cheri!"

~Clarence M. Rivette, President, Global Perspective Consulting

"*Dynamic Relationships* allows for a shift to creative and innovative thinking and being. It uses the Appreciative Inquiry philosophy and approach to focus on possibilities, inspire creative thinking, reach for aspirations, and connect with our strengths and opportunities in our relationships."

~Cindy Savich, Owner, Baskin-Robbins Store

"*Dynamic Relationships: Unleashing the Power of Appreciative Inquiry in Daily Living* takes an important step toward reconnecting our personal and professional lives by acknowledging the central role of relationship building. Stavros and Torres have put together a powerful toolkit to help us impact change in all of our relationships through a paradigm shift from problem-solving to Appreciative Inquiry. Through the AI-4D cycle, we learn how to become fully aware of our intentions and choices, and to see how reflecting on our actions, reframing our questions, and suspending our assumptions together can reveal a world of possibility for sustaining positive change."

~Trena M. Paulus, Ph.D., Educational Psychology Department, University of Tennessee

"This book really gets to the heart of the matter—what happens to us in our lives is because of our relationships with others. Learning to live in an appreciative paradigm calls for a time out to reflect and consider how our actions impact others. It is an easy and enjoyable read that gets you engaged from the first few pages."

~Marji Czajka, Wife and Mother of Nick, Jessie, and Jake

"Stavros and Torres do a brilliant job of teaching us how to keep an appreciative direction in our lives and relationships. They offer a thorough, insightful, and inspirational look into the underlying dynamics of how we can go on together in positive and powerful ways...truly, a life changing book."

~Jacqueline Kelm, author of, Appreciative Living

Dynamic Relationships

Unleashing the Power of Appreciative Inquiry in Daily Living

Jacqueline M. Stavros
and
Cheri B. Torres
Foreword by David Cooperrider

Taos Institute Publications
Chagrin Falls, Ohio

DYNAMIC RELATIONSHIPS
Unleashing the Power of Appreciative Inquiry in Daily Living

COVER ART: What a powerful image of dynamic relationships the ocean expresses. At the macro level, the ocean represents the unseen paradigm in which all ocean life exists. The currents and the ocean's relationship with the elements above and below it affect the animals and plant life of the sea without their even knowing that it is present. The ocean itself is in relationship with the planet and the other elements of our world—the wind, the sun, and the land. When the earth quakes in the depths of the ocean, the sea responds and a swell that gathers the force of a powerful tidal wave devastates the land and all that inhabit it, in turn impacting the human condition and inspiring our capacity for compassion and courage. When the full moon rises, the tide responds. At the micro level, when the winds blow hard and the sun shines hot, the ocean transforms itself, one drop of water at a time to fill the air with vapor, which becomes clouds, then rain, where drops of water once again become part of their whole.

SECOND PRINTING 2006

FIRST EDITION
Copyright © 2005
by Jacqueline M. Stavros and Cheri B. Torres

jstavros@comcast.net
cheri@mobileteamchallenge.com
or www.dynamic-relationships.com

Taos Institute Publications
Chagrin Falls, Ohio

ISBN: 0-9714416-6-9
LCN: 2005931580

PRINTED IN U.S.A.

THE

Introduction To
Taos Institute Publications

The Taos Institute is a nonprofit organization dedicated to the development of social constructionist theory and practices for purposes of world benefit. Constructionist theory and practice locate the source of meaning, value, and action in communicative relations among people. Chief importance is placed on relational process and its outcomes for the welfare of all. Taos Institute Publications offers contributions to cutting-edge theory and practice in social construction. These books are designed for scholars, practitioners, students, and the openly curious. The **Focus Book Series** provides brief introductions and overviews that illuminate theories, concepts, and useful practices. The **Books for Professionals Series** provides in-depth works, which focus on recent developments in theory and practice. Books in both series are particularly relevant to social scientists and to practitioners concerned with individual, family, organizational, community, and societal change.

Kenneth J. Gergen
President, Board of Directors
The Taos Institute

Taos Institute Board of Directors
Harlene Anderson
David Cooperrider
Robert Cottor
Kenneth J. Gergen
Mary Gergen
Sheila McNamee
Diana Whitney

Taos Institute Publications Editors
Harlene Anderson
Jane Seiling
Jackie Stavros

Executive Director
Dawn Dole

For information about the Taos Institute visit: www.taosinstitute.net

Taos Institute Publications

Focus Book Series

The Appreciative Organization, (2001) by Harlene Anderson, David Cooperrider, Kenneth J. Gergen, Mary Gergen, Sheila McNamee, and Diana Whitney

Appreciative Leaders: In the Eye of the Beholder, (2001) Edited by Marge Schiller, Bea Mah Holland, and Deanna Riley

Experience AI: A Practitioner's Guide to Integrating Appreciative Inquiry and Experiential Learning, (2001) by Miriam Ricketts and Jim Willis

Appreciative Sharing of Knowledge: Leveraging Knowledge Management for Strategic Change, (2004) by Tojo Thatchekery

Social Construction: Entering the Dialogue, (2004) by Kenneth J. Gergen and Mary Gergen

Dynamic Relationships: Unleashing the Power of Appreciative Inquiry in Daily Living, (2005) by Jacqueline M. Stavros and Cheri B. Torres

Books for Professionals Series

SocioDynamic Counselling: A Practical Guide to Meaning Making, (2004) by R. Vance Peavy

Experiential Exercises in Social Construction – A Fieldbook for Creating Change, (2004) by Robert Cottor, Alan Asher, Judith Levin, and Cindy Weiser

Dialogues About a New Psychology, (2004) by Jan Smedslund

For on-line ordering of books from Taos Institute Publications visit www.taospub.net or www.taosinstitute.net/publishing/publishing.html

For further information, write or call: 1-888-999-TAOS, 1-440-338-6733, info@taosinstitute.net or taosinstitutepublishing@alltel.net

A Note From The Editor

Dear Readers:

I lost my partner in editing this book because Jackie Stavros, my co-editor, joined with Cheri Torres in writing *Dynamic Relationships: Unleashing the Power of Appreciative Inquiry in Daily Life*. She took on the role of co-author while I, with the support of Kenneth Gergen, Harlene Anderson, and Dawn Dole, was the editor of this most fascinating and powerful *Focus Book*. I see this book as a new area for the *Focus Book Series* of the Taos Institute Publishing. Past writings in the series have focused on change in groups, organizations, and even whole cities.

The *Focus Book Series*, based in social construction, suggests that it is important for us to pay attention to "how we are in relation with one another," because this very thing significantly influences what we create and experience together as shared reality. Thus, *Dynamic Relationships* offers an opportunity to look inside personal relationships as significant to social construction. I acknowledge this book may be a challenge. I ask you to try it. Take time for cycles of reflection and action. Experience what they say and how they feel. Indulge in reading the book. You will also learn from their offering of deeper explanations around the Principles of Appreciative Inquiry (AI)—and learn of the Principle of Awareness as key to living the essence of the Constructive, Simultaneity, Poetic, Anticipatory, and Positive Principles. The principles described in this book also apply to leading change efforts with individuals, with teams, or across divisions, organizations, and communities.

AI has been traditionally used for organizational innovation and cultural transformation. The book was originally intended for those readers who want to *sustain* AI within their organizations and *extend* and *elevate* AI beyond organizational life. This includes learners in undergraduate and graduate courses in leadership, organization development, organizational behavior, organizational change, and collaborative learning. The second audience includes those who are new to the AI concept; yet believe in the power of dynamic relationships as key to enriching and balancing personal and work life.

You will see that *Dynamic Relationships* is focused on individuals-in-relationship with others. It offers ways and means, through the "Let's Put It to Work" sections, to help you to develop habits of thought and action that support your quest for positive relationships. The book calls for a shift to creative and innovative thinking and being, made possible through living in positive relationship with others. It uses the AI philosophy and approach to focus on possibilities, inspire creative thinking, reach for aspirations, connect with your strengths and opportunities, and tap your thinking capacity based on expanded relationships in both your personal and work life. I encourage you to become partners with Jackie and Cheri in using AI to live in dynamic relationship with those who are meaningful in your life. I did!

Sincerely,
Jane Seiling, Senior Editor
The Taos Institute Focus Book Series

To my dynamic co-author, colleague, and dear friend, Cheri, for her faith, deep and uplifting conversations, unconditional love and support. To my husband, Paul, two children, Ally and Adam and my parents for theirs.

Jackie

To my collaborative partner, friend, and colleague, Jackie, with whom it has been and continues to be a delightful journey into what it means to unleash AI in our lives that we might generate positive dynamic relationships. To my husband, Michael, my daughters, Laura and Carmen, and my mom for learning along with us. And in loving memory of my father.

Cheri

Table Of Contents

Foreword

The world is venturing into a new paradigm in which we *consciously* co-create meaning in our world. With these exciting words, Jackie Stavros and Cheri Torres offer us a wonderful volume for learning to live into the appreciative paradigm as well as ways to unleash the positive resources for change that lie omnipresent in our relatedness to everyone and everything that exists.

The key is recognizing the dynamics of our relationships and the significance of our actions, and then living with appreciative intent, say the authors. It is all about unleashing the "true", the good, the better, and the possible—tapping into the universe of strengths—with elevated and ever expanding awareness, in every encounter and relationship. And "yes" it is something that can be cultivated, easily. In many ways, say the authors, we as human beings are born to appreciate and to express love, to see the best in others and in turn to reap the benefits of others' appreciations of who we are and might become. *Put most simply: relationships come alive where there is an appreciative eye, where people are able to see the best in one another and create new visions together— with the desire for building not just new worlds but better worlds.* There is a sense of adventure in what the authors are proposing here. The perspective they speak about is literally limitless in its applications.

A short time ago, just as one example of the significance and relevance of this, I shared some of these ideas at a leadership conference. The presentation was apparently well received, as one could sense from the buzz in the room. And then a senior executive of a Fortune 500 company came up to me immediately after the talk. I will not forget his words. He said:

> These ideas have implications for every aspect of our business— for literally everything we do as a business…but I only wish I had heard these ideas when I was raising my children.

Surprisingly, little has been written on applying Appreciative

Inquiry—or "AI" as it is increasingly called—in one's life. And this is the achievement of this terrific book! While the literature on AI as a constructionist approach to organization development is burgeoning, precious little has been written *about* AI beyond the workplace to the family, the carpool, the children's athletic or art groups, the community, or wherever we gather to connect or play or collaborate. The significance of this is profound, because to really sustain AI in our communities and organizations, propose the authors, we need to practice AI in the more inner and intimate areas of our daily lives—ongoing, a way of life, not just an episodic organization development or change management project.

This work is unique in that it translates complex concepts and research into easy to understand language, exercises, daily experiments, and expansive questions for personal and cooperative reflection. There are applications of recent breakthrough research that is taking place in the positive psychology movement, positive organizational scholarship, and social construction. For instance, here is one example from Chapter 2 that is easily understood:

❑ Pick one person each day and find something to compliment them for. The compliment should be sincere and genuine. For some, this will not be a stretch. It is something you have thought but not said out loud. Choose a different person each day; be adventurous and choose people with whom you are not usually in the habit of socializing or working. This is especially powerful if you choose someone who says, asks, or does something that doesn't fit your frame. Pause and reflect before responding the way you are immediately inclined to respond. Look for the gift, insight, creativity, or beneficial perspective they are offering. You might even pick complete strangers. When you have seen the "gift" in their perspective or through their eyes, compliment them in some way for it. Ask for nothing in return, and watch the effect your compliment has on the person. More importantly, reflect on what effect your shift in understanding has on your relationship.

I will tell you what happened to me when I did this exercise. First, it changed my questions. Instead of our normal problem-solving state which can limit us by focusing on everything that is "wrong" and can narrow our attention to available "fixes", I had to pay attention in a fuller, appreciative way: *what is it that is best, most worthy of compliment and gratitude that I see in the other?* Secondly, with this question guiding me, I started to learn—I saw things in Hannah, my daughter, I had not noticed nearly enough. Hannah is in high school and I was amazed by her provocative thoughts on the political dynamics during the U.S. Presidential elections. When I really listened to her—at one point she asked "Daddy, if we have such a large impact in the world and if we believe in democracy, why don't we let people around the world have a voice and vote in our election?" Instead of jumping in to explain why not, I paused. I began to see her as a young adult with leadership potentials I had scarcely noticed. My compliment back to her was to share how *her* remarkable thoughts and questions changed my teaching the next day at the University and how she made me think about how proud I was to be a citizen—a world citizen! How she lit up! Next, right after the compliment exercise, she started asking me new things about my work and field. That night, she asked if we, privately, could talk about some tough things happening behind the scenes at school with people she had trusted and thought were friends. I felt sadness in the things she shared, but was overjoyed by the opportunity to talk, to relate, to bond father-daughter. A mini-miracle happened, the gift of each other in a vital developmental sense.

This is not trivial. Carefully embedded in this micro-social chain reaction is an upward spiral theory of change. We make our world significant. This book shows that

1. By the courage of our questions (the deep search for what is best in life and the strengths of those around us), we change the world around us,

2. It is in the depth of our connections and conversations with others that we change ourselves and our relationships one conversation at a time, and

3. This happens through the relational resources that are born and shared in settings of mutual appreciation and discovery that results in fostering love, empathy, hope, inspiration, respect, and joy.

If you choose only one of the dozens of exercises in this book, please don't overlook this one. We literally live in worlds our questions create. Hannah and I will never be the same. Why? Because I am going to repeat and repeat the exercise until it becomes, as the authors suggest, a new and automatic action—an "appreciative action."

As I say, this is the first book to bring Appreciative Inquiry straight into our personal lives. I hope it is the start of many more, for the appreciable world is so much larger than our normal appreciative capacity for knowing it. Walt Whitman once said, "As for me I know nothing else but miracles"; guess what Whitman could see? He was aware of poetic possibilities everywhere. This is what Jackie Stavros and Cheri Torres get us to understand: that it is a conscious choice. *Dynamic Relationships: Unleashing the Power of Appreciative Inquiry in Daily Living* will help all of us unleash unexpected positive change everywhere we apply its life-centric principles.

David L. Cooperrider, Ph.D.
Professor of Organizational Behavior
Weatherhead School of Management
Case Western Reserve University
Cleveland, Ohio

Acknowledgements

Dynamic Relationships: Unleashing the Power of Appreciative Inquiry in Daily Living exists because of the great deal of time and depth of conversations from many people. The efforts that we wish to acknowledge took place over the course of the last several years. First it was the idea, then the conversations, next the development of our dynamic relationships, then nearly two years of writing, more challenges, and finally the book itself took on a dynamic shape of its own. The conversation of Appreciative Inquiry at a personal level began many years ago with David Cooperrider. He provided us the relational pathway to this original concept of living an appreciative life. We have heartfelt thanks to David and his colleagues at Case Western Reserve University, especially Suresh Srivastva and Ron Fry. Thank you for your seminal research and being our teachers. We also thank board members and associates of the Taos Institute and the founders and co-owners of Appreciative Inquiry Consulting for their contributions to this field of practice.

We acknowledge the direction, commitment, and collaboration of the Editorial Team from the Taos Institute for shaping this book: Kenneth Gergen, Harlene Anderson, Jane Seiling, and Dawn Dole. They saw pathways we did not and coached us along one conversation at a time. For making this a reality, most *sincere* acknowledgements must go to Jane Seiling, the senior editor of Taos Institute Publishing. Once this proposal was accepted she never left our side. Her voice and editing guided us through another twenty versions of the manuscript. Her capabilities, dedication, concern for quality and feeling for the reader made a difference to every chapter. She accepted our emails and calls any day and any time. Thanks also for the creative book and cover designed by Paul Stavros and David Runk's production team at Fairway Press. That team, comprising Missy Cotrell, Production Coordinator, Rebecca Brandt, Bethany Sneed, and Beth Diamond were instrumental in the formatting and design of the text; Jennifer Bible was responsible for the final cover design.

Others whom we wish to single out for their help, insight, editorial comments, and encouragement along the way include: Marilee Adams, Patty Castelli, Ivy Gordon, Sue Hammond, Joep C. de Jong, Bobby Forshell, Rich Henry, Paul Hilt, Jackie Kelm, Bernard Mohr, Trena Paulus, Kim Porter, Mike Rinkus, Clarence Rivette, Dan Saint, Cindy Savich, Marge Schiller, Jacqueline Sherman, Carolyn (Rainey) Weisenberger, Susan Wood, and Sue Wyatt. Each of you helped to elevate our work and reflect on our words. Thank you to those who helped to edit this manuscript in its final stages: Stan Baran, Ed and Martha Kimball, Barbara Kouskoulas, Patrick Riney, and Paul Stavros. We are grateful for a special gift of *Relational Identity*, a poem by Patrick Riney. We are immensely grateful to each of you for the precious gift of your time, expertise, and support.

We are grateful to Jackie's colleagues and students at Lawrence Technological University College of Management who supported this book from start to finish in many different ways—thank you for your commitment, enthusiasm, and insights. We fully appreciate the times that many of you listened patiently and politely about the status of this book. It is through writing and teaching that you learn and through learning that you write and teach! Cheri took time to visit with many of the MBA and DBA students throughout the last two years to engage them in Appreciative Inquiry and Experiential Learning. The students would ask just the right questions at just the right moment. We are also grateful to the faculty and students in Cheri's cohort in the Collaborative Learning Doctoral Program at the University of Tennessee for engaging in dialogue that informed this book: John Peters, Trena Paulus, Annie Grey, Ron Bridges, (Laura) Rong Li, and Cynthia Ghosten.

Finally we thank our families for giving up so much of us during our dedicated writing time. Creating a book of this focus and depth requires the unconditional love and support of the people with whom we are closest in our lives. It has been wonderful to invite our families into this manuscript and our relationship. They have encouraged us, provided honest feedback, engaged in many of the exercises, generated ideas, and given us the opportunity to engage in positive dynamic relationships. We especially wish to acknowledge with love and appreciation: our husbands, Paul Stavros and Michael Torres, and our children, Laura and Carmen Torres, Ally and Adam Stavros. Thank you to our parents, Stan and Fran Baran, Ed and Martha Kimball, and Barbara and Joseph Bogert (who began the journey with us) for their enduring support and love. We have been affected in pivotal ways by our relationships with all of you, which bring home the very heart of this book. We are deeply grateful. *Dynamic Relationships* is what it is because of our shared journey.

Relational Identity
By Patrick Riney

We
Are who we are
Until
Someone views us
As someone other
Than who we think ourselves to be.
Instantly
We become also
Who we seem to be to them.
It's true,
As society's children
We are so much more
Than who we are to ourselves.
We also are
Who we are
To everyone else.

Prologue

"We cannot live for ourselves alone.
Our lives are connected by a thousand invisible threads,
and along these sympathetic fibers our actions run
as cause and return to us as results."
~Herman Melville~

This book is designed to open the doorway into the *appreciative paradigm* in daily living. It describes how living with the intent to create positive, expansive ways of relating and knowing actually increases the sustainability of positive change in and beyond previous applications of Appreciative Inquiry (AI) to organizational life. *Dynamic Relationships* invites you to unleash the power of AI in your life, influencing the generation of communities that construct positive meaning. It will also influence your way of being in the world.

This book is about living Appreciative Inquiry. It is about seeing yourself in relation to and integrated with whole communities. We use this venue to offer the practice of the principles of AI as the foundation for being in relationships. Living AI requires enhancing awareness through cycles of reflection and action:

- *Reflection* calls us to ask questions such as:
  Q. How are we responding or reacting to one another?
  Q. What are we aware of (assumptions, beliefs, thoughts, feelings, etc.)?
  Q. What are we working to create and how are we creating meaning together?
  The hope is that this might lead to further reflections like:
  Q. How did I come to understand things the way I do when it seems so different from you?
  Q. How can we come to understand one another and create shared meaning?
  Q. What meaning will my actions have for others?
  Q. How are my actions influencing the relationship?

- *Action* calls for [or includes] consideration for the options I choose. Such consideration addresses the impact my choices have on the environment and others; the way my action changes the relationship or community; and the impact of my actions on my relationships, my organization, or family.

When we recognize and understand the dynamics of relationships, we discover new ways of knowing or understanding, new ways to be in relationship with the world and everyone in our life. We have the opportunity to generate more joy and abundance in our lives by relating in appreciative ways. This book is about entertaining the possibility that our lives and the world in which we find ourselves cannot be held apart from our reflections or actions. Ken Gergen suggests that by "reflecting critically on our taken-for-granted worlds, and the way in which our lives are affected by these constructions, we may be freed to consider alternatives."[1] *Dynamic Relationships* is about considering and choosing to work with the appreciative paradigm. It is about entertaining the idea that we are inseparably related to one another and that by relating with positive intent, we can create more effective and joyful communities.

The *appreciative paradigm* is a perspective that invites us to attend to the positive dynamics in our relationships and communities:

Q. What is working?
Q. What gives life to the relationship?
Q. What is right?
Q. How are we successful because of our dynamics?
Q. How can we achieve our greatest dreams together and discover our positive core?

This paradigm calls us to recognize that we are relational beings: we do not act alone in the world, and every action has a relational impact. This book is a personal call to become aware that *you are integrally related with others*—including us, the authors, as you read this book—and that you are a part of creating meaning in the world through your actions and interactions with others. Further, it is a call for you to have a positive impact in all of your various communities of choice—with significant others, family, friends, communities, organizations, and beyond.

Who Should Read This Book?

We invite anyone interested in creating and sustaining positive change in the world to join us. We intend the term 'community' to be understood in the broadest sense of the word. We understand community to include the intimacy of your relationship with your partner, the small community of your family, the larger community of friends and neighbors, your community of faith, your communities of learning and education, your work community, as well as any other group with whom you share an interest and a relationship. In the smallest sense of community, we include your relationship with yourself; in the grandest sense of the word, we include the world. Your immediate communities; however, are those with which you relate on a daily basis. It is in these relational communities that positive change in the world is potentially constructed and sustained.

We have written this book for those who have experienced AI or some type of strength-based approach to change and want to sustain it at work by seeing the impact of it in daily living. Yet it is relevant for anyone who wants to *consciously* have positive dynamic relationships in their life. For those new to AI, we invite you to read more about its origin and use in organizational life. The reference list at the end of this book includes a wealth of resources, though reading these is not necessary to gain value from *Dynamic Relationships*. For everyone it encourages you to embrace life by recognizing your connections and the inherent relevance and value of your actions.

What this book calls for may require a significant shift in your perspective. It requires leaving a paradigm that may be familiar and comfortable, one that may have proven highly successful for you. The current dominant western worldview, which espouses rugged individualism, autonomy, independence, and progress through problem-solving, has delivered wealth to many (you may be one) and incredible technological advances for the world (which have benefited many). We have been influenced by this cultural paradigm as well as participated in continuing to reinforce it by the way we live. This individualized paradigm is part of the way we frame our world, how we understand, and how we make decisions. This book is about re-framing how you see and experience your relationship to your communities and the world.

Dynamic Relationships is a call to change the way we live and work together. It is an invitation to develop a new set of beliefs for how you perceive and make sense of the world. It is also intended as a guide for a new way for all of us to make meaning together. Many corporations, communities, and families are doing just this as they flatten their structures. They are seeing themselves as dynamic systems and calling for leadership at every level because of the value of engaging the full potential of every person.

The idea of systems thinking has been around for more than 50 years in the engineering and scientific world. Jay Forrester is responsible for introducing the concept of systems thinking to organizational change in the 1960s. He suggested that an organization was a complex whole of interrelating and interdependent parts, stressing *relationship* as the process that created the context of the organization. Peter Senge is responsible for bringing this concept into the public forum with *The Fifth Discipline*. Steven Covey's *The 8th Habit* calls for the awareness of *real* relationships as the critical factor for the power of an organization. Organizations are networks of relationships between people. This power is the connection between the people, the quality of relationships.

The shift is spreading to communities that are calling for their members to have a voice, to recognize their relationships are dynamic, and to take an active role in creating their community of choice. Families share decision making in family meetings where children can be heard. This book is about sustaining such positive change by supporting your ability to recognize the dynamics of your relationships and to act with appreciative intent.

What's in This For *You?*

Imagine a life of opportunity, one full of possibility and potential. Imagine a life where you have a sense of wholeness and connectedness with others. This kind of connection is fluid, positive, enriching, and dynamic. It is a life where anything that can be imagined has the potential to be developed and brought into being. Imagine celebrating conflict as a catalyst for discovering diversity in knowledge and opinion as well as differences in underlying assumptions. Ponder the value of such collaboration in the generation of new knowledge and innovative thought. Consider the resulting value to your organization and to the world. Imagine families relating in ways that make them strong, whole, and mutually supportive, acknowledging strengths in differences and celebrating individual gifts that make the whole so much more than each person alone. Imagine feeling alive, vibrant, curious, empowered, safe, valued, and joyful—the sense of life that a young child has, but recaptured with the kind of awareness that only an adult can develop.

Does this sound too good to be true? Our experiences of taking appreciative action in our communities affirm that such a world is possible, and there are people who are moving toward it already. You may even know some of them or know *of* them. You may have said, "They're so lucky" or "I wish I were more like them," never imagining that it is possible for your life to be different. There is nothing stopping you from moving towards this imagined world except you and your way of making sense of the world. As soon as you can see and accept that you have options in creating a meaningful life, that you can perceive, interpret, and act differently from the way you are right now, you have the option of moving toward the world you imagined.

Moving toward your imagined world is a gradual process, simply because it calls for changing old habits of being in relationships. We cannot predict how long it will take you to step into this promising world. We, ourselves, are still moving toward it—but we can predict that you will experience moments of what you imagined as you practice the exercises and complete the journal assignments that you find throughout the book.

Positive dynamic relationships are based on six core principles explained in Chapter 1. The more dedicated you are to practicing these six principles, the more you will experience relationships that uplift and elevate. Be encouraged that it is a continual process of moving toward the appreciative paradigm where your actions are governed by positive intent. With every step—no matter how small—you will be moving in that direction. But don't take our word for it, try it yourself. If you do, as David Cooperrider suggested in the *Foreword*, you will not be disappointed. In fact, we predict you will be delighted.

This book is about discovering your current habits of thought and action and—with awareness—learning to be in relationships with appreciative intent. You will find exercises, activities, journal reflection questions, and other ideas to support your ability to live into this new paradigm. Your ability and dedication to living in the appreciative paradigm will be determined by your willingness to try the activities, practice new ways of thinking and acting, and apply each principle in daily living. The principles are[2]:

1. The Constructionist Principle—the way we know affects our actions.
2. The Principle of Simultaneity—change happens the moment you ask the question.
3. The Poetic Principle—life is an open book.
4. The Anticipatory Principle—we move in the direction of the images we hold.
5. The Positive Principle—the more positive the image or question, the more positive the action.
6. The Principle of Awareness—self-reflective awareness is needed to apply the principles in your life.

The concept of *Dynamic Relationships* is based in large part on the groundbreaking work of David Cooperrider and his colleagues into what has come to be known as Appreciative Inquiry (AI). Therefore, Chapter 2 of this book introduces the five core principles of AI and the new Principle of Awareness. We explore the ways that these principles enhance relationships and sustain positive change in families, organizations, and communities. Deciding you want to engage consciously in dynamic relationships is easy; transforming the way you relate and living the six principles requires change. It calls you to question assumptions, change old habits, beliefs and values, and entertain new perspectives. This is the challenge we address in Chapter 3, where you will learn a technique to develop self-reflective awareness regarding the dynamics of your relationships and expand the possibilities for what can be created in those relationships. In this chapter we bring in the concept of the *collective person*, as developed by Jane Seiling. In Chapter 4, we share a useful framework for bringing the power of AI into your life through the practice of appreciative intent. Chapter 5 provides key illustrations and exercises to help you sustain positive change in daily living. Chapter 6 is our closing invitation for you to join us in seeing the world from the appreciative paradigm in hopes of changing our world—through dynamic relationships!

How to Get the Most Out of This Book

There are a couple of ways to read this book. One way is the standard approach, where you start at the beginning and read straight through to the end. This approach will give you the big picture, after which you can go back and begin to practice the exercises and ponder the questions. The second technique is to read a chapter or section of a chapter and then experience what you have read by answering the questions or doing the activities sequentially as laid out in the book.

To get the most out of any book you must act—and, in this case, maintain an ongoing determination that doesn't wax and wane. Thus, we offer the following suggestions for nurturing that determination:

- *Work with a partner or collaborative learning group:* Find another person or group and form a Dynamic Relationships collaborative group (a DR partner or group). DR partners or groups should be others who are interested in positive dynamic relationships, systems thinking, and discovering new ways of making meaning in life, specifically using a strength focused, appreciative approach. You can even develop an on-line dialogue with a cohort of people who are collaborating to bring about a new way of relating in their department or organization. If you prefer to work on your own, we encourage you to use a journal as your DR partner. It is important to allow other voices to surface in your journal assignments by imagining how your colleagues, friends, and family might respond to a given question. Listen to these voices and reflect deeply on your experiences. It is valuable to do your work in relationship, even if it is in relationship with yourself and the many perspectives you can imagine.
- *Practice and live the six principles:* Applying these will change your relationships and your world as you know it.
- *Act:* Do at least one activity a week, preferably one every few days.
- *Reflect:* Pay attention to your thoughts and actions—reflect, and be aware of how the world reflects back on your actions. Be aware of the options that arise when reflecting on your thoughts and actions. Be aware of the possibilities that you and others have, and when possible explore these options together.
- *Be curious* about the dynamics of relationships and how it is that people bring about the best in each other in any situation.

If you follow these five suggestions, your world will change, most of your relationships will improve, and you will discover a whole new sense of freedom. You may find that friendships deepen and expand, and you may also loose friendships. There is much to be gained by sharing experiences, discovering each other's stories, and having support for a change process. We would never have discovered and learned all that we have if we had not been in dialogue with one another, as well as with all those who have given valuable feedback and insight on this book. If you join us in this dialogue, together we will discover and learn even more about positive dynamic relationships. We invite you to work with us in discovering all the positive possibilities we can create together in coming to know what it means to live in dynamic relationships with appreciative intent.

Co-authoring this book has been challenging, enlightening, exciting, energizing, and rewarding. Though we began our conversation about writing together in 2003, we did not understand fully what we would create together until its completion. It has truly been an experience of collaborative learning and emergent knowledge, sharing our hopes, insights, and assumptions. What we have experienced through the process is what happens when Appreciative Inquiry is unleashed in dynamic relationships. This book truly is a living testimonial of what is contained in its pages.

Asking each other to explain and clarify helped us move beyond our assumptions and tacit understandings. Defining concepts and ideas coherently enough to write them could only have happened in collaboration with one another and others. It meant discovering the dynamics in our relationship and learning how to maximize our strengths in our work together. Those who reviewed our early manuscripts asked questions that challenged our views and pushed us to go deeper in our understanding. In doing so, our way of knowing and speaking about what it means to live in the appreciative paradigm were transformed. This book is by no means the final product on this paradigm; it is the beginning of an exciting new adventure.

Finally, as authors and learners, we invite your comments on this *Focus Book*. We invite you to join us on this collaborative journey by sharing your stories and giving us feedback. Your comments on what you read and how you are applying it in your life will contribute to the emerging knowledge pool associated with dynamic relationships and appreciative action. With your insight, experience, and input into the process everyone learns more. Please contact either of us at jstavros@comcast.net or cheri@mobileteamchallenge.com or www.dynamic-relationships.com.

Jackie and Cheri

Chapter 1

Introduction

"Change always starts with confusion;
cherished interpretations must dissolve
to make way for the new."
~Margaret Wheatley~

The incredible challenges facing today's countries, organizations, communities, families, and individuals, as well as our global and environmental problems, require creative solutions. They require us to recognize the dynamics of our relationships and to work constructively with the dynamics of those relationships. They require innovative thinking generated through enlivened and motivated conversation. We need an approach that focuses on possibility, inspires creativity, and taps our full thinking capacity. This is the appreciative paradigm in action.

The Origin of the *"Appreciative Paradigm"*

A paradigm is a model or way of understanding or representing something. Thomas Kuhn brought this term into public use with his paradigm-shifting book, *The Structure of Scientific Revolution.* He defines a paradigm as a set of beliefs that govern the way the world is perceived and understood. A paradigm is a way of organizing and explaining what is happening (in your world), which is governed by a set of (spoken or unspoken) rules or principles.

The *appreciative paradigm* is so named because of Appreciative Inquiry (AI), one of today's most recognized and popular approaches to systems change. AI is being used by thousands of companies and communities around the world to undertake change initiatives, including companies like McDonald's, NASA, Hunter Douglas, Tendercare, Roadway, and community organizations like Imagine Chicago, Imagine Nepal, the United Nations, Girl Scouts—USA, Save the Children, and World Vision. Systems change can be large scale—like Chicago, Nepal, or NASA—or small—like a family or a relationship. The appreciative paradigm is applicable to them all.

AI is "the cooperative search for the best in people, their organizations, and the world around them. It involves a systematic discovery of what gives a system "life" when it is most effective and capable in economic, ecological, and human terms."[3]

To appreciate is to simply value something. It's the act of recognizing the best in people and things. It is also to increase in value.

To inquire is the act of exploration or discovery. It also refers to the act of asking questions and being open to seeing new potentials and possibilities.

At its broadest level, AI is about discovering value in people, places, and things. It is about discovering the positive core. These are the strengths, life-giving forces, and the greatest opportunity in a situation or an organization's process of discovering and moving toward even greater value. AI is a way of embracing life that gives hope and opportunity to each day and every situation. A fundamental concept related to AI is that every person, place, and thing has something of value, some worth, some untapped opportunity; one simply has to inquire into it. The appreciative paradigm is a model for living that encompasses AI and its principles.

Since we use the word "positive" throughout this book, we feel it is important to provide you with *our* understanding of the term. We use 'positive' as Kim Cameron and Arran Caza define it, as "referring to an affirmative bias focused on the elevating processes and dynamics."[4] In using this point of reference we understand that the dynamics of these elevated feelings, processes, and outcomes generate communities with increased capacity for learning, innovation, creativity, critical thinking, and collaboration. We propose that relating with such positive intent creates dynamic relationships that expand our capacity to respond to the challenges of our world.

The Problem-Solving Paradigm

We are born into the world without boundaries or lines of separation between us. Research on early childhood development has led to the conclusion that infants do not experience *I* and *Thou*, but rather they simply experience. They explore the world through touch and taste. "What is this?" "What does it taste like?" There is little regard for safety or fear of harm as infants and toddlers explore the world with curiosity and wonder. Language development pushes a child's inquiry further into the world. They question, "who, what, where, when, how, and why, why, why?" A young child's interest is simply about exploring and experiencing; they naturally ask learner-oriented questions. "What can I do with this?" "What happens if I do that?" "How does this work?"

Their unbridled curiosity and experiential drive are curtailed in the name of safety, language development, and socialization. Staying safe in order to stay alive becomes a primary focus. Learning to fit in and behaving in socially acceptable ways become the primary lesson. The child comes to make sense of the world through language that frames us as distinct individuals and develops a foundation for relationships which is associated with you and me, right and wrong, winner and loser, safe and harmful, etc.

For generations children have developed within a framework of differentiation, separation, limited resources, and the concepts of competition and danger. They have been encouraged to be careful to judge the comparative value and safety of everything. "What's wrong with this picture?" "Which one is different from the rest?" "Am I good enough?" "Am I better than?" "Be careful of the dark." "Don't smoke, don't drink, don't run, and don't speak unless spoken to." This type of questioning and thinking leads us to inquire into the world around us in ways that focus our attention on what is different, what separates us, what is wrong, and what needs fixing. This leads us to judge all that we experience. We call this approach *deficit inquiry*; it leads to deficit-based solutions to problems.

As a perspective for moving forward in the world, such inquiry has been useful. Society reflects incredible advancements: inventions and improvements, highly successful corporations, technological and medical advances, and scientific discoveries about the nature of living cells. Individualistic deficit-based thinking informs the very foundation of our thinking process and for most people it is hard to imagine a different way, much less a better way. Along with all of the benefits; however, we have generated striking divisions among groups of people in the world. We are a nation divided, a world at war, and a planet threatened by environmental crisis. The cost of individualism, competition, autonomy, and deficit-based inquiry is immense.

Shifting Paradigms

Current research in psychology, education, science, and organizational behavior raise important questions about the merits of looking at the world solely in this way. Such research suggests that a different way of understanding the world is essential. The notion of dynamic systems is now showing up everywhere. This notion is that nothing happens in isolation, but rather every change—even a small one—results in an instantaneous shift for everything that is related to that which changed. With this realization comes the opportunity to ask questions about how our actions actually impact our relationships and communities.

This is a different way of inquiring into and being in relationship to the world. It offers even greater potential for planning, growth, education, improving relationships, and innovative change. Current research in the field of Positive Psychology is finding that focusing on what is wrong in an effort to fix it actually narrows our thought repertoire, thereby restricting our access to the very skills we need for creativity and critical thinking.[5] Engaging in activities, thoughts, and behaviors that produce positive emotions, for example, uncovering what *is* working and dreaming about the ideal, actually expand our thought repertoire and increase creativity.[6] Greater capacity for change, growth, learning, effective relationships, and solution-finding is the outcome.

This is not to say that there is no place for the traditional problem solving approach. When the electricity goes off, we celebrate the electrician who can figure out what is wrong and fix it. But inquiry into deficits does not serve us well when our goals are to develop trust within relationships, educate our children, or create innovative change within an organization or political system. Deficit inquiry is actually an obstacle in such situations.

A simple example may provide clarity. Senior management has called for your department to "do more, faster!" (A novel idea, eh?). You have met with your department several times and looked over your entire process searching for ways to eliminate wasted time, energy, and resources. You have streamlined to the fullest extent. There is nothing more that can be cut without jeopardizing the end result. Your team has looked for all the possible ways to fix the system (as it exists) and there is nothing more to be done. Management says, "Not good enough! Do more, faster! Our competition is doing it twice as fast for half as much money!"

Being the bright, intelligent, person that you are, you realize that if someone else can do this faster and better, so can your team. You recognize that you have been given a benchmark and realize that this calls for innovative change. You now address the situation in a completely different way with a different set of questions. You move into an inquiry. Your first question to management is, "What exactly is it that you want us to do more of and faster? Tell me what you really want." Based upon the answer, your second inquiry then, is "how can we do 'that' in the fastest way possible, with great results?" Now your team comes together around an entirely different project. You have a different goal and you are free to bring the combined creative capacities of your team to achieve that goal. This time you allow yourselves to move toward the actual goal, instead of trying to make an old process do what it can't do. Your solution will undoubtedly look quite different from the one found via old process of deficiency. The nature of your questions must change; the solution is integrally connected to the vision.

Stepping into an Emerging Paradigm

Dynamic Relationships is about stepping into this emerging paradigm. As noted earlier, we refer to it as the *appreciative paradigm*, where we come to make sense of the world as a dynamic system and we relate in appreciative ways. This paradigm is based on recognizing that everything is integrally related and these relationships are governed by a set of six principles. These six principles include the five original principles of AI—the Constructionist Principle, the Principle of Simultaneity, the Poetic Principle, the Anticipatory Principle, and the Positive Principle—plus a sixth principle, which we introduce: The Principle of Awareness. We believe self-reflective awareness—*people's aware of their relationship to others in a community*—is essential to unleash the full power of AI in your life.

To explain dynamic relationships, we offer the following definitions. The first two are dictionary definitions; the third is taken from systems design work related to civil engineering:

> **Dynamic:** *characterized by continuous change, activity, or progress; characterized by vigor and energy.*

> **Dynamics:** *the physical, intellectual or moral forces that produce motion, activity, and change in a given sphere; the conduct of an interpersonal relationship.*

> **Dynamic Relationship:** *a model where objects in a design are aware of their relationship to other objects in the design; make a change and the entire design updates and changes automatically. The objects are products of the design and automatically react to changes in the design. It is a model rather than a static entity. With dynamic relationships, design changes and "what if" scenarios can be done faster and in multiple iterations to see how the changes affect the site design.*[7]

Thus, we offer you the definition used in this book:

> **Dynamic Relationships:** *Communities where members are self-reflectively aware of the richness of their relationship with and to others. Their awareness extends to understanding that relationships are dynamic; any action taken on the part of any member will result in changes for other members and potentially for the community as a whole.*

Furthermore, dynamic relationships imply that the members of the community can impact the whole system by their actions and they, as part of the system, will similarly be affected by the actions of others in the community. Dynamic relationships mean that community changes and "what if" scenarios can be accomplished fast and in multiple ways when responding to the challenges or opportunities presented to the community.

The addition of AI into these relationships allows the underlying intent behind actions to progress in the best way possible for the community and to increase value by relating in ways that generate elevated feelings, processes, and outcomes. We refer to relating in this way as living with *appreciative intent*. Dynamic relationships governed by appreciative intent will inevitably lead to appreciative actions by members, resulting in greater participation, joy, happiness, and value. Taking appreciative action in your relationships is living the six principles with positive intent. From the appreciative paradigm such actions are natural.

Whenever new paradigms emerge, they emerge across many disciplines and social sectors. The most current research in psychology, education, medicine, and organizational scholarship, reveals dialogue and learning that reflect the appreciative paradigm. This research assures us that we are indeed significant players in creating meaning and generating knowledge in our associations. We act and create change and we are changed when others act. Our actions within our communities are generative. Quantum physics tells us that, at the most detailed level, the universe is less a statement about what *is* and more an invitation to *probabilities*. Current research in physics indicates that "material stuff" is really more a probability statement that is highly correlated with not only what is going on the instant before it is observed or measured, but also with what happens the same instant that the observation or measurement takes place. What *is* is inherently relational and dynamic— it is connected through time and space.

We are relational beings, integrally connected to one another and our environment. our relationships deeply inform who we are and how we act, which in turn impacts others at "this moment"—

impacting the "next instant" in the relationship. Our actions and their impact on others are inseparable. We are interconnected. This is the very nature of dynamic relationships. Our collective experience today determines what our tomorrow will look like. The appreciative paradigm suggests that changes in our relationships and communities come about through our conversations—the words we choose to use, the questions we decide to ask, and the way we hear and understand the answers informs our thinking and knowing.

This means we play an integral part; we are a link. Most significantly, how we choose to interact in a relationship matters. This concept explains why traditional problem-solving inquiry—with its focus on comparative-judging questions—is likely to lead us down a path towards an awareness or outcome very different from the path resulting from questions based upon discovering, valuing, imagining, designing, and learning.

Judging questions set us apart from the situation and result in statements that lead to deficit-based answers (what is wrong, who is to blame, how could such a thing have happened?).[8] Such questions imply and reinforce individualism and separation; as Parker Palmer says in *The Courage to Teach,* "either-or-thinking has given us a fragmented sense of reality that destroys the wholeness and wonder of life."[9] "What is wrong with 'that'?" or "What is wrong with him?" implies a very different kind of relationship than "What strengths does he bring to the group?" or "What aspects of 'that' are working well for us?" In the first sense we look for the misfit, why something or someone is not part of the community. We seek solutions in the other rather than in the relationship. In the latter case we are looking for the fit, how something or someone enhances the community or our process; how it or they fit into the *whole.* In this way we seek solutions through relationship. In actuality, the extent and breadth of the research supporting the appreciative paradigm tells us self-reflective awareness is essential to living together in ways that bring joy, abundance, and wellness to our organizations, communities, and families on an on-going basis because our relationships are dynamic.

As significant members of a community, our actions very quickly become a responsibility. This responsibility requires our full awareness, not only of our part in the whole, but also in how our part impacts others, how others impact us, how we want to be together, and what we want to create together. When we no longer see ourselves as standing alone, apart, and separate, our every action becomes significant, because we understand ourselves as integrally related to all that is around us.

Whether we want to or not, as relational beings, each of us impacts those around us in important ways. Our actions are part of creating and recreating our relationships with everyone everyday. The probability of any given outcome for those relationships is in part dependent upon us. Palmer encourages us to "find our place in the ecosystem of reality, that we might see more clearly which actions are life-giving and which are not—and in the process participate more fully in our own destinies, and the destiny of the world."[10] If our action makes someone's day great, we are likely to have a very different interchange with him (or her) than if our action "gets him (her) before he (she) get us."

The process of applying self-reflective awareness requires the following three steps:

1. Pause for a moment, step back, and consider the actions you are about to take and accept responsibility for your part in the dynamics of your relationships with your family, your friends, your colleagues, and your community.

2. Consider the likely impact of those actions on others. How are they likely to respond? What other possible actions might you take and with what consequences?

3. Discover the meaning of your words and actions (as others understand them) by listening carefully and attending to what comes back to you—the responses from others to your actions.

This cycle of reflection and action—based upon active awareness—is what characterizes relating from the appreciative paradigm. This simple yet powerful process changes everything.

In the appreciative paradigm we accept that we are relational
beings and that, by staying actively aware, we can act together
in ways that increase value for everyone. This paradigm offers
significant benefits for accepting responsibility for our lives and
social systems. It calls us to relate in ways that work for all those
involved. Instead of the world happening to us, we happen *with* the
world. A wonderful example of this is presented by Harlene Anderson in *Conversation, Language, and Possibilities: A Postmodern
Approach to Therapy*. Anderson explores the question of how
"therapists and clients can create relationships and conversations
that allow both parties to access possibilities where none seemed
to exist before." She emphasizes the importance of "therapist and
client engaging in *collaborative relationships* and *generative conversations* to form *conversational partnerships* toward powerful
transformations in people's lives and toward successful futures."[11]
This describes a relationship where those involved are aware and
work together to create meaning that is positive for both people.

Dynamic Relationships is about learning to step into this appreciative paradigm to become both aware and responsible and to
subsequently relate in ways that develop healthy, vibrant relationships in communities that are able to create and re-create themselves in effective ways. It's about changing your actions and the
nature of your listening. Our experience is that this paradigm prom-
ises an increasing ability for all of us to generate more joy, abundance, and wellness in our lives, families, organizations, communities, and the world.

Appreciative Inquiry in Action

AI offers a profoundly pragmatic and effective frame for the appreciative paradigm, which is both simple and straightforward. AI
is about inquiring into what is of value, what is working when we

are at our best. Such inquiry as a way of making meaning together generates positive images and positive actions.

Within the field of organization development and change management, a methodology (known as the 4-D Cycle)[12] for creating innovative change using AI has been used effectively, offering a proven approach for positive change. This way of relating at the organizational level has been positively impacting strategic planning and change management initiatives for more than 25 years. Sustaining that positive change is a major challenge for most organizations. A short experience of AI is typically profound for people; however, it is easy to slip back into old ways of relating because of our habits of thought and action as well as established relational patterns. For an organization to truly shift to the appreciative paradigm and to sustain an appreciative way of organizing, a significant number of people must work and live from the appreciative paradigm and its core principles. They must organize with self-reflective awareness as a dynamic community. This will be the focus of Chapter 2.

An appreciative organization or a successful, on-going positive change effort within any system (be it a business, community, church, or family) requires those within the system to live and work within the appreciative paradigm. They must be responsible for creating value, supporting best practices, and building relationships that uplift the members and the organization. When an entire organization or community is aware of the positive dynamic possibilities for working together anything can be achieved. When they do work together utilizing the principles of AI, the entire community will experience greater joy, happiness, respect, and value. Sustaining positive dynamic relationships requires members of a community to practice ways of connecting, relating, acting, and being together that are congruent with appreciative intent.

FOCUS BOX

In closing Chapter 1, we offer a couple of reflections:

☐ Think about someone—from different perspectives: Think about a family member—preferably a spouse, partner, child, or someone with whom you live or work. First, reflect on the things about that person that you would like to fix, change, or adjust in some way. Imagine trying to help them "be a better partner or person" by telling them how to fix or change those things you believe need fixing or changing. Now answer this question: How will they hear your suggestions? What will they experience? How does this thinking inform your relationship with them?

Now think about that same person. This time, reflect on the things about that person that you love, the things they do that warms your heart, the things you appreciate most about this person, the things he or she does really well. When is he or she at his or her best? Imagine telling this person what you respect, admire, and understand about him or her at his or her best. How will he or she hear these acknowledgements? What will he or she experience? How does this thinking inform your relationship with them?

☐ Pause Before Acting: When you are at home tonight pause and reflect for a moment before you interact. (If you live alone, pause and consider your time spent with yourself.) What kind of interaction do you want to have with those at home? Consider what kind of evening you want to have with others. Are your anticipated actions likely to support the kind of interaction you want to have, the kind of relationship you seek?

Chapter 2

Bringing AI Principles Into Daily Living

*"How you imagine the world
determines how you live in it."*
~David Suzuki~

Appreciative Inquiry (AI) was developed in the early 1980s by David Cooperrider and his doctoral mentors, Suresh Srivastva and Ron Fry, at Case Western Reserve University, while working on his dissertation on physician leadership at the Cleveland Clinic Foundation, a large healthcare system. He began his research by interviewing physicians to discover their biggest successes and their biggest failures. As David was completing his data analysis, he noticed that he was drawn to the stories of success. David's wife, Nancy, an artist, brought to David's attention the notion of the "appreciative eye" perspective in art. The "appreciative eye" sees the value, the unique beauty, or the gift in something—often something that otherwise might not be discovered.

David liked this idea and transferred the concept to the organizational world. He discovered that when asked about their successes, the physicians he was interviewing became animated and excited, describing their work with terms that reflected optimism and hope. This was strikingly different from their responses when describing failures, where they'd been noticeably irritable, negative, and physically tense. As he continued his research in the hospital, he found that simply by changing the nature of the questions he asked to an "appreciative" stance, he could create an environment that supported a more positive and hopeful vision of the future for the Cleveland Clinic. In addition, the shift in questions seemed to heighten energy, enthusiasm, and motivation in this huge physician-led hospital system. At that time, they coined the term appreciative analysis to describe this new way of looking at organizational behavior.

This was the first organizational application of what has now become known as Appreciative Inquiry. In the early stages following David dissertation, the appreciative paradigm emerged through his collaborative work with Frank Barrett, John Carter, Ken Gergen, Jane Watkins, and Diana Whitney. These colleagues worked with David to bring this new positive approach to the forefront of organizational development and change.

The AI learning community has been growing steadily ever since. Thousands of people around the world are advancing the theory and practice of AI that is part of a shift in the social sciences toward more constructionist and positive approaches to research, organizational development, and global change. Today, AI is used in diverse global settings and communities and has been shown to be one of the most effective approaches for organizational transformation and learning. It is being used by hundreds of organizations undertaking change initiatives. Such organizations range from government agencies to the military, from leading international corporations to global conglomerates and nonprofits, from school systems to community planning organizations.

More traditional organizational change approaches concentrate on identifying problems and fixing them. AI, in contrast, is founded upon systems thinking, on dynamic relationships in the organization; it seeks to discover the best in human systems and organizational designs. By discovering what makes an organization work well and then applying these practices to other areas within the organization, practitioners have been able to generate significant advances in creativity, knowledge, innovation, and spirit in the workplace. In May 2004, AI received international acclaim as the Distinguished Contribution Honor Award to Workplace Learning and Performance by the American Society of Training and Development (ASTD).

Sustaining those positive changes requires membership awareness that relationships in the organization are dynamic and that appreciative intent on the part of the community is what creates the successful organization. The remainder of this chapter focuses on the principles of AI and how to apply these principles in daily living in order to sustain positive change.[13]

Putting AI to Work in Your Life—Its Core Principles

AI rests on five foundational principles, originally articulated by David Cooperrider and Suresh Srivastva.[14] The practice of these principles in daily living is compelling; when applied with self-reflective awareness, they will lead you to experience their relevance in creating great relationships and success in your organization, community, and family. This book defines and applies these principles at a personal level as well as introduces a sixth principle, the Principle of Awareness. This sixth principle is woven throughout the process of bringing the appreciative paradigm into our personal lives.

1. The Constructionist Principle[15]

The first foundational principle of AI simply states that the way we know (understand) is fateful. That is, understanding and making sense of our experiences impacts our decisions and our actions. For example, if we think someone is condescending we respond differently than if we believe them to be meaningfully coaching us—that their intentions are an offering of care. This is the nature of dynamic human relationships. Our way of knowing or understanding interactions generates positive (or negative) meaning and energy in our organizations. We are always co-creating our communities and organizations through our relationships, our actions, and the norms we establish. Subtle changes in actions, like body language, word choice, or intonation, result in changes in our relationships and potentially the entire community. How we come to understand the world around us and how we are understood by others are fundamental to what we are able to achieve together.

This principle suggests that no matter what the history may be, people and relationships are dynamic; they can thus be open to new developments and possibilities. Simply put, words and actions and the meaning we place on them create our world through language, conversations, and interactions with others. It is in the dialogue and conversations, the interchange of our words and perspectives that we generate the present and the future. Since our actions make the difference, we owe it to ourselves and our communities to act with self-reflective awareness.

A simple example will clarify what we mean. Imagine your supervisor comes to you and in what you sense to be an irritable tone demands to know when the project on which you are working will be completed. Your response and the direction of your relationship with your supervisor depend upon how you understand your supervisor's original communication. You might interpret the words (and body language) as an unjustified attack on you and respond defensively, further escalating negative emotions and potentially damaging the relationship. On the other hand, you might interpret the comment with the assumption that a more senior level manager has just put pressure on him and he's irritated at the manager not you. With this as your way of knowing you might show compassion and support in your response—enhancing the relationship and possibly de-escalating negative emotions. How many of us have come home from work tired, frustrated by something that happened at the office and had a spouse or a child make a reasonable request only to have us snap at them, "No, I don't want to do that!" The difference in how our actions are understood makes a significant difference in not only the relationship, but also the way our children grow.

This is what is meant by "the way you know is fateful." This is the Constructionist Principle in action. Being aware of dynamic relationships paves the way for diverse ways of knowing and the many possibilities for action that result.

Let's Put the Constructionist Principle to Work

The activities and reflections in this section invite you to engage the Constructionist Principle and become aware of the many ways you can interpret and perceive. Each activity below engages you in ways that develops awareness and helps you recognize many possibilities for choices in language and action. This provides you with the opportunity to actually experience the effects of your actions (or potential actions).

❑   Learning from Other People's Experience: We all have situations that leave us feeling challenged and stretched. For this exercise, choose a problem or challenge that is not emotionally charged for you. Find three to six people who you perceive to have successfully met this challenge (or solved this problem). Ask them how they solved it, avoided it, managed it, or surmounted it. You will begin to develop a repertoire of actions and relational patterns that support dynamic relationships. Here are a couple of examples:

o   You want to have a relationship with your kids that does not leave you feeling impatient or frustrated. First, reframe the challenge in a positive way, i.e. you want to develop a relationship with your children based upon patience. Identify three to six parents who show great patience with children. Ask them how they do it. How do they sustain that patience even when it has been a bad day and they are tired or irritable from work? Ask them how they see their ability to be patient impacting their relationships with their children in positive ways. What words do they use in those challenging situations? What actions do they take that help the relationship grow and thrive?

o   You want to stop procrastinating with major projects at work because it creates problems for others and yourself. First, the positive reframe might be: you want to work on major projects in a timely way making sure they get done in a quality manner, on time and without rushing so that the whole team works better. Now identify three to six people who seem to do this well. Interview them; find out how they do this. How do they manage to do all the little things that seem to crop up and take their attention? How do they stay on task? How does what they do impact their relationships with colleagues at work?

❑   Social Group Impact: Try this for one week. Carry around a small note pad and each time you have a significant interaction (over 15-30 minutes) with someone write down his or her name on your pad—use one page per day. If you happen to be a teacher, pay special attention to your engagements with your students. After their name put a plus sign (+) if it was a positive interaction, a minus sign (-) if it was a negative interaction and an (x) if it was neutral. For best practice, reflect more fully; jot down a note or two identifying the reasons it was positive; what actions—from all participants—supported positive relationships? At the end of each day review your list. How many pluses do you have? Do your pluses out number your negatives? Over time, do you notice more pluses?

Now reflect. Who do you spend time with? What kinds of conversations do you have and what kind of relationships do you create together in each small community? Look at the groups of people with whom you socialize. Are you engaging with people who uplift one another, have "right relationships", inspire you, and encourage you? Do you share uplifting stories and tales about others in your lives? Do you spend time talking about what could be and what is working in your lives? Pay attention to these dialogues. As you are no doubt beginning to experience, these conversations create your future. Remember they are dynamic and can change if you change your actions.

❑   Collaborative Construction: Invite a conversation with your family or your colleagues at work. Consciously co-construct the "best possible day", the best meeting your department has ever had, or the best class environment. Begin the meeting or the day by asking each person what would have to happen for this to be a great meeting or a great day. Then create a mutually agreed upon plan so that all the ideas are incorporated and integrated. Here are a couple of examples:

One Saturday the family woke up and each person had something in mind that he or she wanted to do that day. The question posed to the whole family was: What would you each like to do today?
Dad: *"I'd like to go running and get some exercise today."*

Adam (4 years old): *"I'd like to go on a hike and use our new hiking sticks Dad made!"*
Ally (6 years old): *"I'd like to pick flowers."*
Mom: *"I'd like us to eat a healthy breakfast and replace some of the dead greenery in our house."*

As they shared their images for a quiet Saturday morning looking for ways to make it work for everyone, the morning activity became clear. Ally finally suggested, "Let's eat some healthy cereal, and grab our hiking sticks and I will share mine with mom because she does not have one and climb those hills behind the house where we can pick flowers and find mom those green things for her planters." Their simple images and words became a fun-filled reality. They also changed the way the family related for the day, staying together and yet still meeting everyone's interest.

A group of colleagues working on a project came together for a planning meeting for the project. The question that initiated the meeting was, "What outcomes are we each hoping for in this meeting?"
Ben: *"I'd really like dates to be set for each step in the project so we finish on time."*
Donna: *"I'd like to be clear about exactly what my responsibilities are."*
Bob: *"I'd like everyone to be clear about the budget."*
Patty: *"I'd like it to end by 3 PM because I have another meeting to go to."*

The agenda was quickly outlined with times allotted for each item. Patty volunteered to be timekeeper and everyone agreed they wanted to be finished by 3 PM. They proceeded to move from item to item, achieved each of the desired outcomes, and ended just before 3 PM.

A courageous teacher invites students to help generate the best possible learning environment for them by asking, "How can we create our learning environment together so that you engage, learn, and enjoy this class?"

The class discussion generates ideas from students such as "Make it fun!" "Let us be involved and doing stuff." "Make it relevant to my life, why should I learn this stuff?" "Make it a challenge and then help us learn it." "Make me want to be here." "Let us work together."

The teacher used this information to set up lessons plans that included activities, group projects, class discussions, challenging assignments, and guest speakers that used the subject in their daily lives. Students felt heard and participated fully in class. It was her best class ever.

In all of these examples key elements included a willingness to make room for each person's interest and the desire to work or be together as a group. These concepts supported those involved in listening, respecting, and being willing to create shared meaning.

❑   Speedball: This is an activity to do with a group of people; you will need a timekeeper. The challenge is simple. You stand in a circle. Toss a ball back and forth across the circle to one another. Each person should receive the ball only once. The last person to receive the ball just holds onto it. Repeat the same pattern several times until everyone is sure of whom they are throwing it to and who is throwing it to them. Now you are ready for the challenge: "Now do it for the record. Go for the fastest time for everyone to touch the ball in the same sequential order." (These specific words are important.)

At some point, when the group believes they have the fastest time, give them the record time, which is less than one second. After their initial "Impossible" reaction, they will go on to achieve it.

This is a prime example of shared meaning and how it impacts what is possible for a group. When the participants share an understanding that the way to pass the ball is by tossing it, then they work hard to toss the ball as fast as they can in order to accomplish their goal. Incremental change occurs but is limited. When their paradigm is shaken by the benchmark, they begin to question the meaning of the instructions. They open up to the possibilities for a new understanding for what it means to touch the ball. Suddenly innovative change is possible and they achieve what they thought was impossible.

In debriefing this activity with people, ask them what kinds of information and inquiry supported their ability to see the possibilities for new behavior. For instance, only after hitting a certain speed will the group realize that by changing the size of the circle or rearranging the participants can they achieve their ultimate speed. It is these kinds of questions that support innovative solutions.

Special Note: This is best facilitated by someone who knows the outcome of the activity. Typically group members will begin tossing the ball just as they have been doing and trying to do this as fast as they can. They get a time and then try to beat the time. Eventually they repeat the same thing over and over hoping for a faster time, but they reach a limit. Early on, some groups realize they can rearrange themselves, they can move in close, and they can eliminate many seconds this way. The record for more than 15 people is less than one second. When this benchmark is introduced, innovative thinking immediately begins. People ask for the directions again and they begin to challenge their assumptions. The only way to succeed at this is by finally completely restructuring the way they envision the process. (When asked for the directions or information, simply repeat verbatim the original instructions.)

These activities around the Constructionist Principle will give you a lens into the dynamics of our relationships. As we create meaning together we automatically sow the seeds of action; as we generate meaning together we create the future.[16] Social construction offers insight into why the possibility for co-creating a most preferred future lies in our relationships, where actions based on appreciative intent play out among those in the community and how our words create shared meaning and purpose. Our relationships are dynamic because when we act and/or speak, others are impacted. Therefore, *how* we act and speak is important because of the immediate impact on others. Choose your words and questions with consideration, respect, and care because they have an impact—the moment you utter them—which is the next principle: the Principle of Simultaneity.

2. The Principle of Simultaneity

This principle works in harmony with the Constructionist Principle. It states that *the moment you inquire into something change begins to happen.* Inquiry and change, for all intents and purposes, are simultaneous events. There are no neutral questions or comments. Each question or comment moves a conversation or thought process in one direction or another; the interaction is dynamic. Your comment is perceived by others and interpreted from their frame of reference, and they then respond, moving the conversation accordingly. This cycle is continuous. The key to applying this principle in your life is being aware of the dynamics generated by your inquiry. The responses you get from others let you know whether or not your words and actions are received in the way you intended.

Here's a specific example. Two people are engaged in a conversation about their work in a hospital. One is a hospital administrator who is trying to engage doctors in a project, and he is expressing his dismay at the lack of care and interest on the part of doctors. He is describing, in detail, their apathy and lack of cooperation. The second person has been engaged, with comments and questions like, "You're kidding. What other things did you try to do without success?" Suddenly the second person realizes they are in a deficit-based conversation and decides to change her questions. At the next pause she says, "There must be some doctors who are on board with what you are trying to do, aren't there?" Immediately, the hospital administrator stands a little taller, smiles, and says, "Oh yes, there is a crew of about 15 who are just incredible!" And he goes on to describe all the wonderful things these doctors are doing. They are now engaged in a totally different conversation, moving in a different direction with very different options for engaging more doctors.

Another example, for those of you who have children, is to ask your children, "What was your favorite thing you did in school today?" "What was the best part of gym class today?" Many parents ask their children, "What did you do in school today?" The typical response is "nothing." How can it be that we send children to school for seven to eight hours a day and they do "nothing"? To illustrate the power of this principle, consider this story from a man who is husband, father, and plant manager:

> Although I found the concept of Appreciative Inquiry (AI) interesting, I have not used it fully in practice yet at my plant. However, I have tried a little of it to "test the waters" informally. I recalled from one of the lectures that you had mentioned using AI with your kids on how they approached school. Here is what happened when I tried it out:

> I try to tuck my three children in each night before they go to bed. Their ages are: ten, nine, and eight. I always ask them how their day went and if anything happened at school that day. I get the same answers every time, "good" and "nothing." I've found that I get these same replies, even if they stayed home sick. I have to pry everything out of them. One evening, I asked my oldest son how his day went at school and got the same old reply, "fine, nothing happened." I decided that I would give positive inquiry a try. I asked him "what was the best thing that happened at school today?" I had to ask the question again before he understood what I was asking, and he thought about it for a moment. Then his face lit up and he told me about how they got to dissect a snake and how cool it was, and that their class got a special lunch (pizza) because they had the most reading points. I was literally shocked at how animated he was when telling me

the good things. I would not have known about these moments unless I asked the positive question. Up until that point I was somewhat skeptical about the process of AI and what it could do. Now I always ask my kids, phrasing the questions in a positive manner, how their day went. The answers are like night and day.

If you want to fully appreciate this principle, try something new the next time you find yourself in a negative conversation, the kind where the other person is complaining about something or someone, where you both engage in the "isn't that awful, and then what happened, and how could she" type of questioning. At an appropriate point in the conversation, say something like, "There must be something she does right." Or, "what would you like to see happen instead?" Once you ask such a question, watch how the flavor of the conversation improves, sometimes dramatically. Observe changes in the facial expressions, body language, tone of voice, and language of the other person. Recognize how the relationship itself changes.

The dynamics in your relationships both at work and in other communities change as a result of both the questions you ask and the answers you receive. Seeking value and opportunity helps you learn to ask the unconditional positive question(s) that dramatically alter conversations. These are questions that engage people in telling us about their best moments, things that are going well, and opportunities that may lay hidden in challenges and difficulties. These are questions and comments that elevate relationships and the potential of what might be created through the relationship. Changing the way questions are asked can change the way you see and live your life with others. It literally can change your relationships in a heartbeat.

Let's Put the Principle of Simultaneity to Work

The activities and reflections in this section will help you realize how your words significantly and immediately affect you and others by moving you in the direction of the question that is asked. These activities will also engage you in ways that expand your awareness of this impact.

❏ The "You're Awesome" Exercise: Pick one person each day and find something to compliment about them that surprises even you. The compliment should be sincere and genuine. It may be something you have thought but not said out loud. Choose a different person each day. Be adventurous and choose people with whom you do not usually socialize or work, or you may want to choose someone in your family with whom you want to connect in a new way. This is especially powerful if you choose someone who says, asks, or does something that doesn't fit your frame or way of thinking. Pause and reflect before responding the way you are immediately inclined to respond. Look for the gift, insight, creativity, or beneficial perspective they are offering. You might even pick complete strangers. When you have seen the "gift" in their perspective or through their eyes, compliment them in some way for it. Ask for nothing in return, and watch the effect your words have on the person. More importantly, reflect on what effect your shift in understanding has on your relationship.

❏ Acknowledging Others: Write down a list of the names of your close co-workers, family members, or friends. Next to each one, identify words and questions that you think will inspire and enhance them. Be very specific. For example:

Matt　1. Acknowledge his willingness to support the project in any way that he can.
2. Recognize that his strengths are in the details.

Paul　1. Acknowledge the work he does around the house.
2. Ask him to help do things that he's good at.

Ally   1. Recognize how she helps her little brother with his homework.

2. Thank her for her patience and helpfulness.

Now, practice having a positive impact on those you listed. This is not about manipulating others through false praise; it is about looking for what is best in a person and attending to those things that create great relationships. This will help you recognize that your actions can bring about a positive state (erect posture, eye contact, engagement) through your communication. Be genuine. Discover what kinds of words encourage, inspire, motivate, and enhance others. Finally, commit to doing what you've written with each person every day. It is important to be sincere and honest and to let your words stand unconditionally. In other words, don't disqualify your inspiration by adding a tagline with a negative perspective.

For example, if you tell your office manager, "Matt, you are going to be such an asset to this project. We really need someone to make sure we are on task and meeting our deadlines." This is entirely different from, "Matt, you are going to be such an asset to this project. We really need someone to make sure we are on task and meeting our deadlines even though it'll feel like you're a nag."

Or, if you say, "Paul, the front yard looks great! You've done a wonderful job with the trimming and cutting." This will have an entirely different effect than, "Paul, the front yard looks great! You've done a wonderful job with the trimming and cutting. When are you going to get to the backyard?"

Try the same exercise with your colleagues at work (your boss, those you supervise, vendors, customers, or strangers on the elevators that you see every day), your children, your students, neighbors, spouse, school personnel, and community members.

❑ <u>Ask and Reflect</u>: Ask questions and reflect on the experience those questions generate. Where do they move the relationship? How does your question influence the conversation? What kind of question is it? Where does it focus attention? What is the result of asking an unconditional positive question? Reflect on your reactions and responses to questions or statements from others.

Inquiry, when practiced in the appreciative paradigm, is a positive opportunity to discover and explore your contribution to a relationship or the future. Change begins to happen the moment the questions are asked. How those questions are posed shapes our relationships and our shared future. In asking questions, take a moment to think about how you can most effectively word them; consider how you can phrase them so they invite participation. Frame your question as a powerful unconditional positive question aimed at elevating the person and the relationship and enhancing value for the organization, community, and family.

There are many ways to understand or interpret any given situation. The way this happens is influenced by our assumptions, history, fears, and dreams in addition to the words used by others. What we focus on and emphasize changes the way we relate with others. This is underscored by the Poetic Principle.

3. The Poetic Principle

If you have ever studied poetry in school, you will easily understand this principle. Do you recall your teacher telling you that any single poem has multiple interpretations? The interpretation depends upon who is reading it, when they read it, how they read it, how they feel when they are reading it, how it relates to their life experiences, and why they read it. Additionally, a poem has layers of meaning. The Poetic Principle suggests that the same is true about our lives. It basically says our lives are like an open book or a poem. A person's life-story, like great poems, is constantly being written, and rewritten, read and reinterpreted. We can find new meaning in old story lines when we ask different questions, see with different eyes, or gain new information. The same is true for organizations, communities, families, and relationships as well as your life history. They are all open books. How we interpret the voices, events, and experiences impacts our lives. What we attend to changes the dynamics and thus changes everything.

You have a choice to pay attention to many aspects in any given situation or experience. For example, you can study poor morale at your workplace or moments of enthusiasm and motivation. You can wallow in the fact that you did not get the promotion or you can recognize the fact that you will have the time now to write that book or spend more time with your family. You can look at the joyful moments your child experiences when he or she stops to look at the bug on the sidewalk or you can be irritated by having to slow down or stop moving. You can have a great day by looking for opportunity and value throughout your day or not–the choice is yours. You can focus on the moments of success, wisdom, competence, and strength in your life or you can tell your story from a place of failure and weakness. The story you commit to has a significant impact on the dynamics of your relationships and the role you feel competent in playing in those relationships.

Christopher Reeve, well-known for his acting role as Superman, demonstrated an application of this principle. Here was a man who had everything: fame, fortune, good looks, wonderful family, and health. In the prime of life, fate turned his world upside down, rendering him paralyzed from the neck down after a devastating fall from a horse. The world watched as Christopher healed. The natural expectation, in a deficit-based world, would be to look at all that he had lost, to feel sorry for him, and to understand if he chose to disappear. He could have created a story about himself where he was the victim, left incompetent and weak. Instead, "Superman" generated a different story about himself. Reeve focused on his own healing, on using his fame and fortune to do what hadn't been done before. He supported cutting edge research into spinal cord rejuvenation, returned to acting in whatever way he possibly could, and became an example and a role model to many people throughout the world. It could have been otherwise. We all can be grateful for the choices he made and how he came to interpret his life situation. He died maintaining this high spirit of living life to its fullest.

The Poetic Principle invites you to recognize that the meaning generated in our conversations—at home, at work, in the community, in the world, and those conversations we have with ourselves about ourselves and about others—depends upon where the point of focus is in those conversations. The Poetic Principle invites us to attend in our dialogues to that which will enhance value and elevate our work together; it calls us to tell the stories that empower positive dynamic relationships.

Let's Put the Poetic Principle to Work

The activities and reflections in this section will support your ability to focus attention on what is of value, on the best, on the opportunities available in your relationships and communities.

❑ The Best Stories of Your Life: Coming to appreciate your personal power and capability is essential to creating positive dynamic relationships. One way to recognize this is to find the stories within you that allow you to experience and remember who you are at your best. What is your positive core? Either journal or think about those people in your life that uplifted you, saw your strengths, encouraged you, and supported your potential. What story did they see about you? How have the strengths and potential they saw in you contributed to the positive things you have done and the successes you have had? How might making this story about who you are when you are at your best be the dominant story that impacts your sense of personal power?

❑ Reframing Practice 1: What's going on at work that seems to have a negative frame or has been labeled "a problem"? Notice what you and others are focusing on around this issue. Look at the challenge again. This time identify the components or elements of the situation that are positive or are working. There must be at least one. How might these elements be useful in moving forward? What is it about that component that enables you and/or your work group to learn, succeed, and grow, even in small ways? What in this situation can be utilized well? If your work situation is influenced by someone you perceive to be a problem, identify his or her strengths (skills, behaviors, talents, passion, positive energy, and/or relationships). What is of greatest value and can be most appreciated about this person in relation to this situation? How can you acknowledge these in a public way? Does the person's situation call for those strengths? Is the person utilizing them?

❑ Reframing Practice 2: Identify a past struggle that you faced and overcame. Now reflect on the event to identify what you learned or gained from the situation. Look closely to see whether it called forth strength from you. What opportunities came your way as a result of using this strength? What happens for you when you *re-story* your past?

Often we cannot see the gifts or opportunities until we move well beyond the struggle. For example, it is hard to see anything good about being fired or going home to find a note from your partner saying he or she has found someone else. However, five years later, when you have the best job you could imagine or have met the person of your dreams, you can look back and admit that you are grateful for that day in your past. When you practice this exercise regularly, you may find yourself responding to any struggle with, "there must be something good in this mess!" And as you look for it, you will, of course, find it.

❑ Rediscovering Important Relationships: List the important people in your life—home, work, and community. Next to each person list all his or her strengths and talents. Identify those things that you love, admire, and respect. Pay attention to these things when you are with these people. Acknowledge them for those gifts they bring to the relationship. Then observe and be aware of changes in those relationships. Take action on your reflection and send that person a note or call that person on the phone.

What we attend to contributes to our subsequent actions. As we act with appreciative intent, we open up new possibilities for relationships and for generating our preferred shared future. By deliberating on our actions, the opportunity lies before us to contribute to and sustain the life we most want. The Poetic Principle means mindfully choosing our actions. Applying this principle to future events is the focus of the Anticipatory Principle.

4. The Anticipatory Principle

As human beings we are constantly planning, anticipating, musing, worrying, imaging, thinking, wondering, and designing. This seemingly passive activity has an impact that is fundamental to the Anticipatory Principle. The Anticipatory Principle maintains that human beings live into their "anticipation" of future events, and that this anticipation has an impact on the people and systems around them.

If you doubt this, just check out the continuous conversations you have quietly "inside your head." Typically, this internal dialogue runs something like, "Hope I get it right this time and don't screw up like I did the last time." "Blast, I did it again, when am I going to get that right?" "Let's see, if I'm going to miss the traffic, I'd better leave early. No I can't. So I'd better take Hawthorne Street home or I'll be in traffic for hours. Oh man, another slow driver. Why can't these people get off the road or learn how to drive at rush hour!" "Why did I say that?" These running dialogues guide us into our future. What if our internal dialogue is focused on what we are continually doing right, or proud of or what we hope will occur? What if it went something like this, "I think my input at the meeting was received in a positive way." "The conversation I had last evening with my daughter was an important, positive turn in our relationship, I want more of them." "I am sure that Steve did a great job with the report today; I'll have to remember to thank him after I read it."

Many of us are familiar with the term "self-fulfilling prophecy." A self-fulfilling prophecy can guide a person toward his or her expectations for blockbuster success or lackluster results. The Anticipatory Principle reflects Henry Ford's famous statement, "Whether you believe you can or you can't, you're right!"

Two of the most common findings of research that support the Anticipatory Principle are the Placebo Effect and the Pygmalion[17] or Galatea Effect.[18] The first of these informs us that what we believe to be true affects our well-being and ability (to heal). For years, doctors have known that under certain circumstances giving a patient a placebo (a pill made from sugar or an inert substance) can cure an illness simply because the patient believes it will.[19] Double-blind studies have further documented that if the physician also believes the pill will cure the patient, the patient is even more likely to be healed. This is known as the Pygmalion Effect and it tells us that what others believe about us affects our well-being and ability to succeed. (It also tells us that our beliefs about others affect their ability to achieve). The power of belief is very strong.

An extremely potent example of the Pygmalion Effect is a simple exercise done by Jane Elliott, a third grade teacher.[20] After Martin Luther King was assassinated, she was determined to find a way to help her students fully understand the impact of racism and how people are easily influenced by what others think or say about them. She set up a school experience so that blue-eyed children had privileges based upon the concept that they were smarter and superior because studies had shown that this was fact. They were given preferential treatment in class and in the lunchroom; they were called on more in class. These students responded positively and they thrived.

She then reversed the treatment. This time the brown-eyed students were smarter and given preferential treatment. Now the brown-eyed students stood taller, raised their hands more often, and found their self-esteem higher. After the experience, students were amazed at the impact that it had on them. They understood the power that other people's beliefs had on their own beliefs and their ability to thrive and develop to their fullest potential. Such is the nature of truly dynamic systems; the connection is so strong that even subtle shifts from any member of a community can change the way the whole community creates itself.

What you believe about yourself and your capabilities impacts your willingness to try, to stretch, to reach your dreams. What you believe about your children, your partner, and your colleagues impacts how you interact with them, which in turn informs their beliefs about themselves. If you believe someone is lazy and needs to be coerced or given incentives to work, you are more likely to interpret their actions and words within this context, regardless of whether or not it is true. (In management, this is known as the Galatea Effect; it is the same as the Pygmalion Effect).

A wonderful example of this occurred in a major trucking company. It took place between a unionized dockworker (let's call him Rick) and his manager (let's call her Linda). Prior to initiating AI into their organizational change process, Rick and Linda held stereotypic beliefs about one another and their jobs. These stereotypes guided how their relationship played out. Rick believed management was out to take advantage of him and his fellow workers. His conversations with Linda were always adversarial. She believed him to be an angry, aggressive, uncooperative member of the union. The tension and hostility between them were noticeable to everyone. They were relating in a static world where there seemed no other possible way to relate. After attending a large group meeting where AI was introduced and used, Rick began to entertain the idea that there might be another way of being in relationship with Linda. He wondered whether Linda might actually have different intentions than he had believed. With his willingness to suspend his judgment of Linda and imagine that it could be different, he discovered his part in creating their relationship. With his opening to the possibility, they stepped into a dynamic relationship.

Things began to change. Rick was more open (though still very skeptical in the beginning). Linda began to see strengths in Rick she did not know were there. She began to ask him for input and give him responsibilities that she would not have dreamed of giving him before. Rick became self-reflective and discovered the world of possibility; he began to see himself differently. He eventually realized how much a static relationship and single-minded expectation had created their former relationship and how it stood in the way of their ability to create something awesome. He is now enrolled in college and has taken on responsibility for helping to deliver AI training and AI summits across the country for the organization. Linda is both delighted and amazed not only at the difference in the relationship, but also at the power of this principle in action. It has changed what they can accomplish together for the organization as well as the experience of working together. And, they are not the only ones having a similar experience in the organization; as the organization has become truly dynamic it has increased its capacity to deliver services and profits have grown significantly.

The power of this principle lies in action. When we act from an expectation, we move towards what we anticipate. Individual anticipation affects our relationships; collective anticipation impacts the direction in which a relationship, community, or organization moves. When we collectively create the anticipation of a mutual goal or vision, we tend to act and support one another in achieving that goal. Generating shared anticipation can be an important element in the success of any undertaking.

Let's Put the Anticipatory Principle to Work

The activities in this section will help you reflect on the expectations you hold for your relationships, including your relationship with yourself. If you approach these exercises open to the many possible outcomes in any given interaction, you will discover the power of the Anticipatory Principle in your daily living.

❑ Setting the Stage: Before your next important discussion with someone, take a few minutes to imagine how that discussion will go. What are your expectations; what are the expectations of other(s) who will be involved? Visualize your behavior and words and see if the others respond in the way that you hope they will. If it is a situation that is creating anxiety for you, take full breaths and imagine the situation is over and it has turned out beautifully for everyone involved. Now "rewind" from that perfect ending and see what happened to bring about that beautiful result. How did you act and speak? How did others respond and how did you react to them? Pay special attention to what you were thinking; what beliefs supported you? Now make those images big, bold, close-up, and colorful.

[Neurolinguistic Programming techniques have demonstrated that when we hold images that are big, bold, dramatic, animated, colorful, and full of other sensory information we are very likely to live into those images. Similarly, if you are carrying such images but they are negative scenes that you want to stop, you can play with the images like you play with a movie camera. First make the scene black and white, then make it fuzzy. Slowly make the images smaller and smaller. Change some of the characters so that they are cartoon-like or make them silly animals. Make the animation silly. Run the scene forwards and backwards scrambling the images each time. Then make the images grow smaller and smaller until you can't see them. Then replace them with positive images.]

❑ Open Dialogue: Before beginning any important dialogue or discussion with others, for example a business meeting (or even planning a family vacation together), ask everyone what their expectations are for the conversation (or the vacation). What outcomes are most desired by everyone in the meeting? Then encourage the group to anticipate achieving those outcomes, meeting everyone's needs. When the community shares an anticipated vision of the future, they are more likely to go there together quickly and effectively. Afterwards, reflect on the power of this process on the dynamics of the relationships and the outcomes achieved.

❑ Expectations Inquiry: Ask others about their expectations for you and/or the group. How do they anticipate the relationship/s unfolding? What roles do they see themselves and you playing in a project? What roles and behaviors do they see in the family dynamics? How do people see you and the others in a community meeting working together to reach the desired outcomes of the meeting? Such dialogue opens the door for not only discovering one another's strengths, but also discovering where differences in anticipated outcomes might have created conflict in the relationship. By creating shared expectations up front, a different kind of relationship unfolds around the completion of the project than might otherwise have occurred. Reflect on your experience with this practice; how does it support dynamic relationships?

The Anticipatory Principle suggests you begin with the end in mind. It is through anticipating the future that we actually generate it. It is worth the time it takes to develop positive images around positive relationships, actions, and results. These images of the future will affect ongoing conversations and relationships, which will inform where we go together.

5. The Positive Principle

The Positive Principle is the idea that the more positive, bold, and dramatic the images we carry, the more likely we are to move towards those images. This means that shared bold, dramatic, detailed images of our organizations, our relationships, our families, our communities, and our futures will support our ability to achieve those images. The Positive Principle informs the other four principles.

- With the Constructionist Principle, you have choice in the words that help to create your world. Therefore, the Positive Principle underscores the need to use positive language and discover ways of knowing or understanding that provide positive images. It is through this shared language that we make sense of the world and when it is focused on the strengths, positive aspects and aspirations of those people and situations in our lives, we know more fully the power of living the appreciative paradigm.
- The Principle of Simultaneity considers inquiry and change as a simultaneous event. The Positive Principle indicates questions about the good and the possible will lead to positive images and actions. In fact, the more positive the question, the more positive the image, the more likely the positive resultant action.
- In relation to the Poetic Principle, the Positive Principle invites us to explore the many possibilities for discovering "good poetry" in any given situation. This principle suggests we attend to the possibility (instead of the problem), moments of joy (instead of sadness), and sources of energy (instead of inertia). Within the Poetic Principle we have choices to interpret our lives and our relationships with a focus of the "positive".
- The Anticipatory Principle says we move in the direction of our images and expectations. The Positive Principle suggests the wisdom in imagining positive actions and holding positive expectations will result in uplifting the world and those around us.[21]

You can experience the effect of this bold imagery right here. Recall an experience that was quite pleasant, one that brought you joy and increased your sense of appreciation or gratitude. Now, bring the image of that experience more fully to mind. Make it big, bold, and dramatic. When most people do this they have a physiological response to it. If your image stayed small, distant, and black and white, you would be less likely to re-experience the feelings associated with the image. On the other hand, if you were able to expand the image, make it full color and close up, you most likely experienced feelings in response to it. The same is true of the images we create for our future. When we create bold dramatic images that evoke feelings, they are compelling; we move towards them.

Sports psychology uses this principle to generate athletic advantage. Understanding we will move in the direction of our images and thoughts (the Positive Principle in action), great athletes visualize their success as part of their practice. Studies have shown that those athletes who not only practice but also visualize success in great detail (including how they are feeling, what they are wearing, exactly how they play, etc.) are more successful than those who simply practice. Outstanding performers spend almost as many hours visualizing their outstanding performance—from beginning to end, including their emotions, their thoughts, their behaviors, and their words—as they do in actual rehearsal or practice. Who would hire an architect to build a building without a blueprint? Who could develop a world-class company without a vision, mission, or plan? How can we shape our families and communities based upon our greatest, strongest, and most positive images of their futures?

In short, deliberating on positive images can affect your relationships with everyone as well as the outcomes for the future. Similarly, developing shared positive images within a community or organization can impact the community and its future success. Living from the appreciative paradigm puts you in charge of creating vivid, powerful, positive images for your future that will compel you to move into them; it puts communities in charge of creating shared and collective visions which inspire them to move forward together. Once we create these compelling images, our actions are more likely to flow from them to generate the reality.

Let's Put the Positive Principle to Work

The activities and reflections in this section will help you practice the Positive Principle in daily living.

❑ Bring Out the Positive: Create situations and choose to be in situations and communities that bring out positive feelings in you, situations, and people that amplify everyone's strengths and talents. First, this requires you to reflect. What are the kinds of situations that elicit positive feelings for you and others? When are you and others at your best? You may enjoy learning and find that a strength of yours is taking in new information. Taking a class would be an example of creating a situation that elicits positive feelings. Perhaps you and your family experience positive feelings when you walk in the woods or see beautiful nature films together. Creating a positive situation might be to schedule weekly hikes where you take digital photographs, which you upload onto your office PC. You can use them as a screen saver or click on a slide show when you need a brief respite.

❑ The Collage Method: Create a collage that reflects the images you wish to have in your life. It might be a life collage or it might be around a very specific concept. One of your hopes might be to be more centered and balanced in daily living and to make time for quiet contemplation every day. You might create a collage that shows pictures of solitude and peace. You might show a silhouette of someone meditating; you might add a sunrise or sunset. You might include groups of people doing peaceful things together balanced with fun. You might then finish it off with some words like "centered" and "I take time everyday." Display your collage in a location where you will see it and it will support your living those images.

❑ The Group Image: Choose one of your communities of choice or practice—significant other, family, at work—and start a conversation that will generate a bold, positive, shared vision of the future for the group. Make sure to get input from everyone. You might even go back to the same group you worked with on the activity in the section on the Anticipatory Principle, and push others and yourself to be very specific and detailed in generating bold, positive images. The more positive and vibrant the image, the more compelling it will be for the group.

Positive image *leads to* positive actions and consequences. The Positive Principle tells us the more positive the image or questions asked, the more positive and long-lasting the results.[22] Carefully examine the questions that you ask yourself, the inner dialogue that prattles in your head. Step up and take charge of it. Research has shown that if your inner dialogue supports the vision and action you want to take by a 2 to 1 margin, then, you will move in the direction of your desired vision. It is upon this fifth principle that AI builds its positive framework.

These five principles are in effect in our lives regardless of whether we are aware of them or not. We have an impact on our relationships because *we are our relationships*. Everything that we do and say moves us and those around us in one way or another. Our being is defined by our relationships. In order to appreciate the dynamics of our relationships and live by these principles effectively—in ways that develop healthy, vibrant relationships; however, we must be fully aware—self-aware and socially aware.[23]

6. The Principle of Awareness

We propose the addition of the Principle of Awareness as an essential principle for bringing AI into your life. If you want to experience dynamic relationships in the appreciative paradigm, you need to practice living the AI principles with *self-reflective awareness* of the significance of not only your actions and the actions of others, but also the many possibilities for how the interactions can play out. Self-reflective awareness is not just a superficial or intellectual understanding about the other five principles. It is a stepping back and seeing yourself in relationship to others; it is an experiential awareness of the intersection of the principles and your way of knowing and being in the world.

Self-reflective awareness means being self-aware, other aware, and socially aware of the dynamics of the relationships in a community. It means understanding your part in dynamic relationships, recognizing there are options for your actions that will influence the relationships and that at any given time there are many possible outcomes for any given situation depending upon your actions. Self-reflective awareness implies that the actions you take are considered and taken with appreciative intent to create positive relationships and vital organizations and communities. Self-reflective awareness allows you to recognize the value of reflection and action and the ability to reflect, act, and reflect again with new or beneficial insight that informs your next action.

The outcome of practicing self-reflective awareness is that you discover that your beliefs and your words have a significant impact on others. In turn, other people's subsequent words have an impact on you. Practicing this principle is the means to fully understanding and appreciating the power of the other five principles and seeing how they are interwoven in the fabric of relating.

Awareness is what supports the broadest and deepest application of the other five principles. If we stay in static relationships with prescribed ways of knowing and relating, at the very best we will minimally experience the impact of these principles. In order to unleash the full power of AI, we must be aware of ourselves as full participants in dynamic relationships, complete with many options for our actions. The Principle of Awareness states that...

Only through the act of "waking up,"[24] stepping back, and recognizing our significance in the context of dynamic relationships, and taking responsibility for our relationships will we be able to fully experience and practice the principles of AI to enhance our families, communities, and organizations.

Acting with appreciative intent is about applying the Principle of Awareness through cycles of reflection and action in every area of daily living. It is about practicing reflection by considering your actions and the responses you get from others as well as your responses to their actions. It is about deliberately acting or speaking with positive regard for the dynamics of your relationships. By practicing *reflection* and *action* you will develop greater awareness—of yourself, others, and the interplay between yourself and others as you generate meaning together. Here is how the Principle of Awareness deepens and expands our ability to live the other five principles:

- Within the Constructionist Principle, it means reflecting before acting (or speaking) and considering the possibilities for your action and the likely outcome for the relationship from this interchange. It means examining the many possible ways of understanding another's actions and being aware of the likely outcome of your subsequent actions. It means reflecting and building awareness after each action in order to apply the Constructionist Principle effectively.

- Within the Principle of Simultaneity, it means asking questions or acting with appreciative intent, understanding and knowing that change will happen the moment you act. The Principle of Awareness applied with the Principle of Simultaneity requires taking a moment to reflect on an anticipated action and to consider how your next action might influence the situation instantaneously; how are others likely to perceive your actions. It also means recognizing that the moment others act, those actions affect you. Self-reflective awareness implies that you reflect upon your assumptions, your frame, and that you become aware of your responses in relation to the actions of others and that you take these into consideration in your next action.

- Within the Poetic Principle, it means paying attention not only to where you place your attention and what you attend to in your conversations, but also being aware of how your attention is being directed by the social systems around you. The media focuses on very specific aspects of events in the world, often targeting the latest disaster or crisis. This in turn influences how we see others in the world and how we experience our global relations. Self-reflective awareness means taking into consideration the point of view and intent behind such influences, questioning assumptions, and making informed decisions about your actions and relationships.

- Within the Anticipatory Principle, it means not only being aware of your expectations and beliefs, but also discovering the expectations and beliefs of others. Self-reflective awareness means taking these into consideration before acting, because the expectations and beliefs of others will influence how they perceive your actions. The direction in which we purposely move in our relationships is co-created though our shared anticipation.
- Within the Positive Principle, it means developing the skills and abilities to act in ways that generate elevated feelings, processes, and dynamics in relationships through continual cycles of reflection and action. As the Principle of Awareness is applied to the Positive Principle, the positive principle is more readily applied to the first four principles. Greater awareness and insight supports the application of the positive principle.

The Principle of Awareness calls us to be self-reflective and actively engaged in our relationships. For instance, remember the sense of excitement and awareness that comes at the beginning of a new personal relationship? This is a good example of this principle in action. The energy exists because we are so engaged and conscious of the relationship and how everything the other person says and does makes us feel. At the same time, we pay careful attention to our actions in order to move the relationship forward in a positive direction. Practicing the Principle of

Awareness allows us to capture this positive energy and sense of aliveness in our relationships. Living the Principle of Awareness asks us to actively:

1. Know and understand that our relationships are dynamic. This implies a willingness to question—ourselves and others—openly with a full desire to understand how we best make meaning together. Such awareness supports our ability to move forward together in positive ways.

2. Step back and reflect in ways that allow us to notice when we are congruent and authentic, when we are practicing what we value in ways that make it obvious to others that we are doing so. For example, we are congruent and authentic when our actions reflect that we want to increase trust in our relationships at work and when others experience our actions as doing just that. They will experience us honoring our commitments, supporting them when they take action even though it may involve calculated risks, and including them in decisions and situations that are relevant to them.

3. Attend to the language we use because it influences our relationships and consequently our communities. Since the words we use create the world in which we live and work (Constructionist Principle), we need to be aware of how our words and actions generate meaning with others. By attending to this through reflection and action, we participate consciously in shared meaning-making.

4. Realize and accept that, as a person living with appreciative intent, we are responsible in all of our relationship communities for our role in elevating feelings, processes, and dynamics with others. This means that we do not blame ourselves or others for "making" us feel or think a certain way. It means we do not make ourselves or others wrong

for our reactions. It means, instead, realizing it is about the relationship, which is dynamic and we are responsible for our part in generating it. In accepting this responsibility, it means making the commitment to reflect on our role(s), see options, anticipate responses, and act in ways that generate effective relationships.

5. Reflect on emotional reactions in ways that support our ability to stay open, be challenged, and give and receive refusals (saying "no") without losing the appreciative direction. Appreciative action does not imply we must always say "yes" or "be positive." It is not the feedback or refusal that is at issue, it is how it is delivered or received. Or, how the action affects the relationship.

6. Be aware of our reactions when someone gives us critical feedback or refuses our request. And, to be aware of how we deliver similar actions. For ourselves as recipients of critical feedback, it is enough to suspend and look beyond our sense of personal judgment to hear and discover the real meaning behind the action or to ask for clarification in ways that help us move beyond our hurt feelings. As senders of such action, it is our responsibility to anticipate reactions and act in ways that support the outcome that has the highest value for everyone. Sometimes we cannot avoid hurting another's feelings because we cannot control their response. However, we can attempt to mitigate those reactions in the way we deliver the message.

The Principle of Awareness unifies and amplifies the other five core principles. Adding this sixth principle brings AI to a personal level and provides the link that allows us to sustain its effects in our organizations, communities, and families. When we live with awareness and appreciative action, AI has the opportunity to move beyond the realm of a positive organizational approach to a wider and deeper application. This allows each individual to unleash the power of AI in their daily living.

The Principle of Awareness works within the other five principles to magnify the effects of AI. Now you see not only yourself in relationship to an organization or community but also your relationship with each individual in that large system. By applying this principle, the impact of AI becomes more personal because you are taking into account all your relationships.

Finally, the Principle of Awareness also helps to extend the effects of AI by providing the participant with a concrete mechanism for keeping it active in their daily lives. By practicing awareness, the core principles of AI begin to live and breathe in our daily lives.

Let's Put the Principle of Awareness to Work

The activities in this section call you to "wake up," be self-reflective and aware, and practice cycles of reflection and action in relationships. Once this journey begins, you will notice subtle changes in what you pay attention to, what you hear and see, how you respond, and the number of possibilities you have for understanding any given situation. Over time the way you come to understand relationships will shift, and you will experience the full dynamics of your relationships. Although this shift is accompanied by a deep sense of responsibility, you may also experience a sense of increasing hope, simply because of your experience of possibility. Our sense of having greater hope is perhaps the best gift of engaging in dynamic relationships with appreciative intent. For hope inspires, motivates, encourages, uplifts, elevates, and anticipates the seemingly impossible.

The Principle of Awareness is an essential and inherent component of practicing the other five principles; by engaging in these exercises you will discover the other five principles in action. Hope comes when you realize your essential connection to the whole—your freedom to positively influence relationships by your actions.

❑ Conversational Awareness: Pay attention to the dynamics of how conversations move in one direction or another. Notice the nature of questions, comments, and statements, and how each of them influences the others in the conversation. What kinds of questions, language, or actions increase positive emotions? Solutions? Conversational joy? Without "playing" with people, test different styles and see what happens. See if you can change the course of a conversation with just one appreciative question. Record in your journal how you have best been able to uplift conversations and move them in positive directions.

❑ Observational Awareness: Observe two or more people in discussion. Assess the general atmosphere of the conversation. Is it relaxed or tense? Does it have a negative frame or a positive frame? Are people smiling and energized? When you watch the body language, are people engaged, leaning in toward one another, making eye contact, and smiling, or are they tight, irritated, and slumped? Note the tone and temper of the voices as well as the actual words. Once you have a general flavor of the energy and atmosphere of the conversation, begin to listen to the language and the words. How do the words inform the other behaviors and vice versa?

Pay attention to the nature of the questions. Are they judging questions or learner questions? What are the participants creating together through their shared dialogue? Imagine what they would need to do to talk about the same subject and create a different experience. What would have to happen? Next, pay attention to the physical responses of others to comments and actions (both yours and other people's). The body won't lie. 93% of communication comes through nonverbal cues: body language and vocal qualities. Only 7% is the result of pure words. Learning to read these important communication cues and communicate them congruently with your words, as well as understanding their impact on you, is important. Be responsible for the impact you have on others.

Think about the kinds of questions you might ask as an intervention that would change the course of the reality-in-progress. (You and your DR Partner might even do this exercise together while having lunch at a restaurant. Listen to and observe another conversation—discreetly of course—and then share your observations, thoughts, and ideas together, or come up with examples from your daily living and discuss the options for positive intervention.)

❑   Evening Reflections: Each evening before you fall asleep reflect on your day. When were you at your best? When were you acting with full awareness and appreciative intent? When were you open to someone supporting your efforts to act this way? When did you catch yourself, see another possibility, and act upon that new knowledge?

Acknowledge your success; allow a sense of gratitude to spread through your whole being, gratitude for those who are supporting you, including yourself. The Evening Reflection can also be used as a Morning Reflection. Before you roll out of bed in the morning recall your successes and ponder a moment how you can increase your awareness today.

❑   Cycles of Reflection and Action: Practice reflecting-in-action, in other words while you are interacting with others, attend to the impact your actions have on them and pay attention to your reactions to what they do. Question the assumptions being made by yourself as well as others. Step back to become aware of the bigger picture and how the conversation is contributing to meaning-making. Try this: set your watch to quietly chime every hour. Then use this to remind you to take a moment to reflect.

The Principle of Awareness is powerful. The first and greatest shift for anyone making any kind of change comes with awareness; those are the "ah-ha!" moments. As your awareness expands through the practice of cycles of reflection and action, you will experience greater and greater opportunity to apply the other five principles. Think about your relationships at work and in your more personal relationships: your ability to engage in appreciative interactions will expand those relationships and provide more significant opportunities for relating in the future. Application of the Principle of Awareness in these relationships will allow you to initiate and sustain positive engagement and change as well as sustain them simply by practicing the principles.

Connecting the Principles to the Appreciative Paradigm

The appreciative paradigm calls us to recognize the dynamics of our relationships, our essential relational nature, and the necessity to act with full awareness, taking responsibility for participating in creating organizations, communities, and families with appreciative intent. This calls for a shift in most people's worldview or frame (of reference). Changing your frame does not happen overnight, however. To believe, accept, and live these principles each day takes time, practice, reflection, and action. Each day that you practice you are *moving towards* the appreciative paradigm.

Appreciative action simply means that the result of your actions elevates people, processes, and systems and searches for the greatest value and worth in any situation. Dynamic relationships are always at work, appreciative action on the part of all members plays a significant role in bringing about the best and most fruitful future for the community. The more everyone leverages his or her energy in this way, the more joy, happiness, and value for the whole. Appreciative actions broaden the capacity of the whole community to learn, innovate, and generate new knowledge collaboratively. Living this way will change your life and your world in positive, meaningful ways. It will also support achievement, success, and the best of human potential.

You will not get there; however, by wishing it so. We are talking about transforming the way you relate to the world. Shifting your paradigm is a challenge, like changing a habit. To change our understanding of what it means to be in relationship and the way we make meaning together will require the same commitment and practice needed to form and maintain new habits.

The exercises under each of the principles are designed to do just this. They will support your change by allowing you to experience options and possibilities where you might not otherwise perceive choice. Doing these exercises does not mean you *will* change your frame. Doing them does not mean you *have* to change the way you understand and participate in relationships. Practicing these exercises will allow you to experience that there is more than one way of understanding your relationships and that how *you* act is relevant in important ways.

For those who experience a sense of insignificance in the world, this is an opportunity to become aware of your significance, to experience its presence. Practicing these exercises will allow you to realize you are making a difference no matter what you are doing. This awareness gives you the freedom (and responsibility) to choose how you make that difference.

You would be well advised to be aware that *doing these exercises will most likely change your life*. In the process, your relationships, in every part of your life, are bound to change. Your perception of who you are in relation to family, loved ones, colleagues, and any other community in your life will change in positive ways. Such changes can be exciting and invigorating, and they can also be scary and anxiety-provoking. If those in your communities are also seeking to live in the appreciative paradigm and you make the journey together, your relationships will be enhanced and nurtured.

On the other hand, if you are attempting this journey solo—and we suggest this is most difficult if not impossible—leaving others in your family and organization in a different paradigm, you may be challenged at times. Sometimes such changes raise questions and fears associated with loss, separation, and alienation. When people no longer find common ground for creating meaning together relationships will not withstand the changes. In many instances, however, relationships will grow stronger—even if at first you are the only one shifting. For this reason, we encourage you to share this book with those in your life who are important to you. Invite them to join you in this exploration of dynamic relationships, ask for their support and encouragement, and offer them yours. Engage in ways that are collaborative—generating knowledge and understanding by practicing the exercises and discussing them together.

This is a journey. Do not think of it as leaving some paradigm and arriving at another. Instead ponder the notion that we are all simply expanding our understanding of what it means to be in relationship. Every action provides an opportunity to live the AI principles. Even if you decide to "go this journey alone," keep in mind that you will not really do it alone; it requires interaction. As your energy shifts in your relationships, those relationships will change and others that are most immediately connected to you will be influenced. When you are working within the six Principles you—and other members of your communities—will discover there is nothing to be lost and everything to be gained. Be patient with yourself. It is a challenge to stay self-reflectively aware at all times. Reward yourself when you have developed the discipline of continuous relational awareness.

In the next chapter, you will learn an exercise that will further support your ability to expand into the appreciative paradigm and change current habits of relating that are problematic. The process will help you develop new habits of action that will support your ability to practice the principles in daily living. When you practice the exercise in the next chapter, you will have the opportunity to manage your reactions and responses to negative stressors that will allow you to witness the dynamics in your current relationships, help you understand how they came to be, and provide options for future actions that allow you to create relationships that flourish.

FOCUS BOX

To summarize the application of these principles in the appreciative paradigm consider this:

❑   In your communities of choice and practice, there is always someone and/or something of value or an opportunity waiting to be discovered.

❑   What you focus on, believe, think, imagine, and act upon informs your relationships and what you can create together.

❑   Your life becomes real and meaningful through your relationships, which arise through your shared beliefs, thoughts, conversations, expectations, and actions.

❑   There is power in asking positive learner questions.

❑   The Principle of Awareness highlights the need for understanding that your relationships are dynamic and you are a significant member of your communities.

❑   The Principle of Awareness supports your ability to apply the original core principles of AI:

> Constructionist Principle
> The Principle of Simultaneity
> The Poetic Principle
> The Anticipatory Principle
> The Positive Principle

And, these six principles unleash the power of AI in daily living.

Chapter 3

Moving Toward Appreciative Action

"Watch your thoughts; they become words. Watch your words; they become actions. Watch your actions; they become habits. Watch your habits; they become character. Watch your character; it becomes your destiny."

~Frank Outlaw~

As we have discussed, practicing the six principles takes more than just deciding that this is what you want to do. It takes developing awareness for the dynamics of relationships and changing the way you relate. Such change requires a change in the way you perceive and make sense of experience, which is integrally related to how you currently make sense of the world and your relationships; essentially, how you know. Recall that in dynamic relationships, changing your actions changes the outcome in your relationships, with the potential to impact the whole community. Sustaining positive change is a matter of engaging in consistent, congruent appreciative action.

Your actions arise from your paradigm. Your present paradigm, whatever it is, has been developed throughout your life as a result of your relationships, especially with family, friends, teachers, colleagues, and the media. This is the Constructionist Principle at work. Moving towards appreciative action means stopping to reflect and consider your present way of acting and reacting to others in your associations (Principle of Awareness) and to consider what actions will positively influence your relationships.

If you take appreciative action, your desire for positive relationships and successful communities or organizations are more likely to come to fruition. The Principle of Awareness calls for you to reflect on your current ways of understanding or making sense of the world and your relationships and then to use new ways of knowing to generate appreciative action. If you've ever tried to develop a new, healthy habit, you know it can be a challenge. Changing the way you know is similar. It is a process of "moving toward" as opposed to an instantaneous event. Like changing a habit, changing the way you know takes commitment, time, and awareness combined with cycles of reflection and action. It requires applying a lesson parents have been teaching their children for years.

The Mack Truck

When we were young, our parents were concerned for our safety, and rightfully so. Things that might do major harm were grounds for yelling, screaming, and otherwise terrorizing us. For instance, when we were about to set foot in to the street to explore more of the world, we didn't see the Mack truck hurtling down the road at 50 mph! We were focused on what was right in front of us; the bigger picture was not a part of our paradigm or worldview. Our parents, however, could see the impending disaster.

For our safety and well being, we were taught how to take in the bigger picture. Our parents taught us to *stop*, *look*, and *listen* before *acting*. What our parents forgot to tell us (or did not realize) was that these words of wisdom were tools that we could use to help us with the metaphorical "Mack trucks" that would come into our life simply because of the nature of dynamic relationships.

Some of those metaphorical "Mack trucks" are reactionary responses like anger, rage, resentment, jealousy, fear, condemnation, and judgment—all negative stressors in our life. These "Mack trucks" seem to come out of nowhere and broadside us time and again, wreaking havoc on our relationships. The truth is they don't come out of nowhere. They come from our constructed, conditioned way of knowing (e.g., judgment, critique, and fear). Negative reactions arise because of the way we understand what has been said or done, which stems from the paradigm governing the way we perceive.

If our way of knowing falls under the structure of a primarily deficit-based paradigm involving rugged individualism, we will look for what is wrong, judge and compare, critique and look for problems, and be on the look out for danger, focusing on "me." This way of knowing, of course, is quite different from ways of knowing in the appreciative paradigm. Developing appreciative actions, which flow naturally in the appreciative paradigm, is a matter of moving from one paradigm to the other. We can begin this process by applying the simple lesson our parents taught us. This lesson will help us step back, raise awareness, see with different eyes in hope of generating more effective relationships through appreciative actions.

Where Did These Habits Come From?

Just how did these habits of action form in the first place? The simple answer is that your way of knowing or making sense of the world has been forming since you were in-utero. Throughout your life the development of your paradigm has been influenced by the people and the world around you. This is the nature of dynamic relationships and the Constructionist Principle. The words and actions of others and your responses, coupled with the consequences of those actions, have brought you to your present way of making sense of the world, your present paradigm for relating and acting. This has been referred to as the *collective person*. It is this collective person, acting in relationship with other collective persons, who creates and sustains relationships and performs tasks.[25]

> The collective person is formed metaphorically like the Mississippi River; the water rushing to the Gulf of Mexico includes droplets that formed at its origin and in tributaries all along the way. The power of the river comes from sources such as the Ohio River and many other small and large rivers and tributaries passing through many states and many other small and large passages from fields and streams along the way. Each droplet merges with others. It would be hard to identify where any drop of water originated...it just came along as the water flowed toward the Gulf. Each person, like the Mississippi River, is altered with each contact, experience, learning, intent, and action.[26]

As a collective person, you have been and continue to be deeply influenced by all of the relationships in your life. The good news is that your experience in and of the world is in a state of constant regeneration as you engage in relationships at work, home, and community; again, this is the very nature of dynamic relationships. Even now, no matter what age you are, new ways of understanding are likely to be forming as a result of your relationship with us through this book. It may be subtle, like a willingness to entertain the *possibility* that there are different ways you might act in any given situation—the first step toward taking appreciative action.

How Does That Happen?

Here we are in the world, ready at every moment to relate. How we react and interact depends upon our perception of the events, relationships, and experiences in our life. The first component of our perception is related to our attention. What is it that we pay attention to? This is the Poetic Principle alive in our daily living. Much of what calls our attention is a result of our conditioned way of knowing, our worldview or frame influenced by how we are feeling, what else we just experienced, our expectations (notice the relevance of the Anticipatory Principle), and any conditioned patterns of relating. If we are not aware of where we place our attention, our attention will be unconsciously directed by our frame or worldview. We will perceive only that which fits into that frame. Here is the importance of the Principle of Awareness. This focus of attention, in fact, is a significant factor in the reality that we experience and the options we see available for relating. If you doubt this, try this challenge:

> Look at the picture below. How many geometric shapes are represented in the picture?

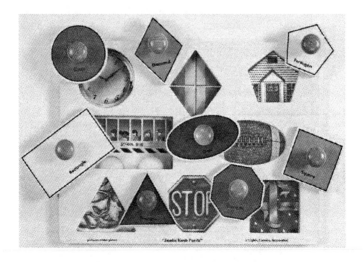

Now without looking back on the previous page, what time was it on the clock? How many children were on the school bus?

We see what we look for and we miss much of what we are not looking for even though it is there. The same can be said of what we listen for. Our experience of the world is heavily influenced by where we place our attention.

As an event occurs, we attend (consciously and unconsciously) to certain aspects of that experience. We make sense of the information according to our paradigm or way of knowing. If our way of understanding what is happening is perceived as threatening, we respond, appropriately, with defenses or other reactions. All of this, of course, happens in a fraction of a second. In some sense it is the collective person—all those past experiences and voices— that engages in this present interaction.

What we attend to and our subsequent actions are also influenced by our relationship with our body and mind in the moment of the experience. This relationship includes our sense of well-being, our mindset (e.g., are we distracted by something or fully present; did something else just happen that is contributing to this mindset?), and the emotional mix that arises in response to the present situation. All of this combines and influences our perception in any given relationship.

Most of what we perceive in our relationships is not "the truth" about them. There are actually many possible perceptions (or truths). How we perceive can be understood within the context of the principles:

1. The Constructionist Principle—how do we know? what is our paradigm or our way of making sense of the present situation?
2. The Anticipatory Principle—what are our present expectations (often governed by prior experiences instead of present and future desires)?
3. The Poetic Principle—to what are we attending; upon what aspects of the situation do we focus?

4. The Principle of Simultaneity—what is the response of our body and mind to the situation, question, or actions of others?
5. The Positive Principle—what is the nature of the images and questions occurring to us; are they positive and bold?
6. The Principle of Awareness—are we aware of all of the above or is it going on unconsciously, putting us in danger of reacting instead of acting?

Since our perception, which is subject to so many variables, heavily influences our actions, it seems important to question or double-check those perceptions for accuracy. For example, suppose you submitted a report to Fred a couple hours ago. You're feeling a little unsure about the quality of the work; it was a rush job. You are also a little annoyed that it had to be a rush job since Fred could have given you the assignment a week earlier but he forgot.

You're walking down the hallway and Fred is coming toward you. You noticed that his brow is furrowed and you think he looks stern or angry. You greet him as he passes. He doesn't respond. You continue down the hallway immediately concerned and then irritated. Your assumption (anticipatory thought): Fred must be angry over the report. It must not have pleased him or he found errors. Now you start worrying about possibly having the boss call you in for a shoddy job on the report. What if you lose your job? And the drama, in your imagination, goes on. Fred, without realizing it, is part of the meaning you have made around this experience. His non-response is the catalyst for your current and future state, and probably the choices you will make the next time you face him or when someone else brings up his name.

Let's rewind the scene in the hallway. What did you actually perceive and what did you do with that information? How did you derive your "story" from the event? First, let's attempt to look at the "facts". You noticed:

1. Fred is walking down the hall; his brow is furrowed.
2. You say, "Hi".
3. He walks past without saying anything when you speak.

But did you pay attention to what he was doing while he was walking? Was he looking at the stack of papers in his hands? Was he gazing into space, lost in thought? Did he show signs that he even noticed your presence? Why did you only notice his furrowed brow and his lack of greeting?

Now consider how you came to understand or make sense of his actions. The story you told yourself; the "truth" you constructed from your perceptions of the interaction. There are a number of other possibilities for how you might have made sense of the "facts". Fred could easily have been so preoccupied with something upon which he was concentrating that he didn't even see or hear you. He could have been worrying about his own issues and was so caught up in them that your "hi" didn't even register. You just gave him the report that morning; he may not even have had a chance to look at it.

Our perceptions and the subsequent stories we make up about interactions are highly influential because of the dynamics of relationships. The representation of the "collective person" is always present. Given all of the pre-existing conditions we bring to our relationships, it is no wonder the "Mack truck" gets us so many times! Remember how, as a child, you didn't think, you just did. When you were running full tilt towards the roadway, someone first had to scream to get you to stop, and then they taught you how to be discerning, essentially by broadening your view in order to see yourself in relationship to the road and the Mack truck!

That same methodology is just as valuable for the metaphorical Mack trucks in life, supporting your ability to move towards becoming self-reflectively aware of yourself in relationship with others. This method is straightforward: stop, then look, listen, and act, applying the six principles. First, stop! Then, look (reflect and apply the principles), listen (reflect and apply the principles), and act (and reflect again).

This process invites you to practice cycles of reflection and action using the six principles in your relationships, beginning with focusing on the "facts" and becoming aware of the assumptions you are making in relationship to those facts. Your reactions and responses happen simultaneously with your assessment of any situation, which is why it is so important for you to stop and reflect before acting.

The benefit of this practice is that it moves you toward the appreciative paradigm. You can discover that you are a significant player in developing positive, generative ways of being in relationship with others. This offers you a means for creating more joy and abundance in your organization, community, and family. As you move towards the appreciative paradigm, appreciative actions will become more second nature.

The Practice

Cycles of reflection and action are essential to taking appreciative action in stressful situations and this practice supports just that. The first step is to do what mama said, "Stop!" followed by inquiring into the interaction: looking at what actually occurred, listening to and considering your responses, and acting only after reflecting on the desired relationship. This is done by practicing the six principles. The process looks like this:

1. The Principle of Awareness: (**Stop**) Take a deep breath.

2. The Constructionist Principle: (**Look**) How am I understanding what has been said or done? How am I making sense of it?

3. The Principle of Awareness: (**Look again**) What is really happening or being said? What are the "facts" and what am I making up? What assumptions am I making?

4. The Poetic Principle: (**Look yet again**) What am I focusing on? What else could I attend to that will provide me with additional pertinent information? How else might this story read?

5. The Principle of Simultaneity: (**Listen**) How did I immediately perceive what is occurring? What state of body or mind contributed to this response and my immediate reaction in how to act? What is my immediate response when I entertain another way of understanding what is currently happening?

6. The Anticipatory Principle: (**Keep listening**) What kind of relationship do we want to create together? What actions on my part will move us toward that kind of relationship?

7. The Positive Principle: (**Act**) What question can I ask that will move our relationship forward in a positive way? What appreciative action can I take?

Ideally this process is carried out in the moment, when you first "see" the proverbial Mack truck in your experience. Before using this process in "real time," it helps to practice the technique by applying it to past situations. You can practice by choosing a situation that occurred in your past where you didn't see the "Mack truck" and you were broadsided, with the consequences moving you away from the relationship you desired.

For example, imagine that last month your department was under a lot of pressure to accomplish a project by a certain deadline. Everyone had been working overtime for a couple weeks and was stressed. If you missed the deadline it was going to be your job on the line. A colleague came by your office to let you know he was leaving for the day. You looked at your watch; it was only 6 PM and you made a nasty comment, shook your head, and made note that this person really didn't care much about the project or the rest of those working there. He definitely would be off the next project.

Here is how the process can play out on this past experience:

1. The Principle of Awareness: (**Stop**) Take a deep breath.
   ➡ *What was that? What just happened? Ahh...*

2. The Constructionist Principle: (**Look**) How am I understanding what has been said or done? How am I making sense of it?
   ➡ *I understood his leaving early as not caring.*
   ➡ *If he truly cared, he would have stayed late like the rest of us.*

3. The Principle of Awareness: (**Look again**) What is really happening or being said? What are the "facts" and what am I making up? What assumptions am I making?
   ➡ *What really happened is he came in and said he was leaving.*
   ➡ *It was 6 PM, already an hour past normal closing time.*
   ➡ *I have no idea why he left when he left; I didn't ask.*
   ➡ *I made up that he didn't care.*
   ➡ *He certainly had worked hard on the project and he contributed significantly to it. In fact, he had stayed later than most every night last week.*

4. The Poetic Principle: (**Look yet again**) What am I focusing on? What else could I attend to that will provide me with additional important information? How else might this story read?
   ➡ *I focused solely on his leaving and the rest of us staying behind and working.*
   ➡ *I might have focused on how much he'd already contributed and how many nights he'd stayed late over the last two weeks.*

➠ *I might have asked if he had plans or if everything was okay at home.*

➠ *I might have even focused on whether I would be more efficient and effective if I left now also and got a good night's sleep.*

5. The Principle of Simultaneity: (**Listen**) How did I immediately perceive what is occurring? What state of body or mind contributed to this response and my immediate reaction in how to act? What is the immediate response I have to entertaining another way of understanding what might be happening?

➠ *I perceived his leaving in a negative way.*

➠ *I was incredibly stressed. It had not only been a long day, it had been a long couple of weeks working on this project.*

➠ *The deadline was looming and I was fueled by fear for my job and primed for reacting.*

➠ *I was extremely tired, hadn't been sleeping well, and knew I was going to be there very late again that night.*

6. The Anticipatory Principle: (**Keep listening**) What kind of relationship do we want to create together? What actions on my part will move us toward that kind of relationship?

➠ *I want a positive relationship with him.*

➠ *He's a good worker, sharp and talented.*

➠ *I want us to relate in ways that are mutually supportive, open, and honest.*

➠ *I want a relationship where we both feel valued.*

7. The Positive Principle: (**Act**) What questions can I ask that will move our relationship forward in a positive way? What appreciative actions can I take?

➠ *I could have said, "Good night, have a good evening. You deserve a night going home early."*

➠ *I could have said, "I know our late nights have been hard on families. Is everything okay?"*
➠ *I could have said, "Thanks for all your hard work on this project; it will be over soon."*

Are you ready to try it for yourself? First recall a past situation where the Mack truck broadsided you, so to speak. Write down what happened and how the relationship evolved through the experience. Then put the six principles to work for yourself:

The Principle of Awareness: (**Stop**) Take a deep breath. What thought or feeling "woke me up?"

_____

_____

The Constructionist Principle: (**Look**) How am I understanding what has been said or done? How am I making sense of it?

_____

_____

The Principle of Awareness: (**Look again**) What is really happening or being said? What are the "facts" and what am I making up? What assumptions am I making?

_____

_____

The Poetic Principle: (**Look yet again**) What am I focusing on? What else could I attend to that will provide me with additional important information? How else might this story read?

_____

_____

The Principle of Simultaneity: (**Listen**) How did I immediately perceive what is occurring? What state of body or mind contributed to this response and my immediate reaction in how to act?

What is the immediate response I have to entertain another way of understanding what might be happening?

_____

_____

The Anticipatory Principle: (**Keep listening**) What kind of relationship do we want to create together? What actions on my part will move us toward that kind of relationship?

_____

_____

The Positive Principle: (**Act**) What questions can I ask that will move our relationship forward in a positive way? What appreciative actions can I take?

_____

_____

_____

The point of this exercise is to understand the application of the six principles in daily living within the cycle of reflection and action, especially under stressful interactions. It also helps you recognize that there are a variety of ways of understanding a situation, often more easily done when you are not in the heat of the moment. Applying the six principles in this way opens the doorway into the appreciative paradigm. It enhances your awareness of your significance in the relationship and invites you to consider appreciative actions in the future.

Repeat and Repeat

To move towards the appreciative paradigm and appreciative actions, practice with a number of past experiences that are over and done. Even though the event is over, such practice will support the creation of new ways of relating. Practice also on current events, perhaps ones where you are recovering from after being hit by the

Mack truck. For these there may still be time to impact the relationship in appreciative ways and to generate new meaning with one another.

The goal, of course, is to apply this practice in real time, when you are in the heat of an event. This is the time to apply mama's rule followed by the six principles.

Applying the Practice in Real Time

If you practice this inquiry process, you will not only begin to see your patterns of response changing, you will come to understand that you have many possible ways of knowing and subsequently acting. You will learn a great deal about the dynamics of your own self in relationship, which should have a positive impact on the dynamics of all of your relationships. With each successful application of this inquiry process in real time you will be moving closer to the appreciative paradigm. One day you will discover that appreciative actions are beginning to come naturally, without much effort. You will have come to understand what it means to be in relationship in a new way. This understanding will impact what you and others in your communities can create together.

This process is based upon inquiry, very specific inquiry. The nature of the questions you have been considering supported your ability to develop appreciative actions. Learning to ask these questions yourself is the subject of the next chapter.

FOCUS BOX

In a normal, interpersonal interaction as soon as you sense the Mack truck—i.e., you become aware of those fast moving negative emotions or thoughts (anger, irritation, annoyance, worry, suspicion, jealousy, judgment, criticism, resentment etc.):

1. **STOP!** and take a deep breath.
   ➡ The Principle of Awareness
2. **LOOK** (reflect)
   ➡ Constructionist Principle
   ➡ Principle of Awareness
   ➡ Poetic Principle
3. **LISTEN** (reflect)
   ➡ Principle of Simultaneity
   ➡ Anticipatory Principle
4. **ACT**
   ➡ Positive Principle

It truly takes practice and time outs to allow for the cycle of reflection and action to move you in a positive way forward in building the most dynamic relationships with appreciative intent.

Chapter 4

Creating Dynamic Relationships

"How we think shows through in how we act.
Attitudes are mirrors of the mind. They reflect thinking."
~David L. Schwartz~

We have focused intently upon the dynamics of interpersonal relationships because we are relational, community-oriented beings. Through our conversations with others we can make meaning in the world and come to understand who we are and what we bring to the world. We are part of an integrated, dynamic, and constantly changing system. There is a paradox associated with this that challenges this new paradigm. Recall the "Mississippi River" metaphor noted in Chapter 3 where we correlated the idea of the individual in isolation with the drop of water in a river. In one sense there is no drop of water when it is in wholeness in its relationship with the other drops in the river. And yet, we can make sense of a drop of water. This is the paradox and it is the same with this new paradigm. In one sense there is no individual-in-isolation because we are a dynamic whole, and yet, we can make sense of the individual. We have a sense of an integrated self—the collective person along with our mind/body experience.

This chapter focuses on the dynamics of this *intra*personal relationship. This is our relationship with our self. We step into this chapter cautiously, for it is easy to lose sight of the continuous influence of dynamic relationships when we instinctively attend only to the self. And yet, whatever we experience as going on for ourselves in isolation is—at the same time—influencing and influenced by the dynamics of past, present, and anticipated relationships. Think of a mirror facing a mirror; everything reflected in one mirror simultaneously reflects not only in the other mirror, but then back on itself. Each mirror is distinct and yet what is seen in the mirror contains the images from the other becoming multiple images of selves. Such is the nature of our individual "self." We are distinct and yet we are, like the mirror, a collective.

In our relationship with ourselves when we reflect on our actions and experience we discover our strengths, stories, and understanding. Often it is in the intrapersonal relationship that we plan future goals and dreams. We decide what we want to achieve; and we engage in inner dialogues that support our ability to achieve goals and reach for dreams.

The same process used by corporations to tap into strengths, develop a vision for the future, and design strategies, plans, and structures to support their success can be used by you for the very same purpose.[27] This process is known as the AI 4-D cycle: *Discovery, Dream, Design, and Destiny* illustrated in **Figure 1**.

Figure 1: The original AI 4-D cycle supports the Affirmative Topic Choice(s).

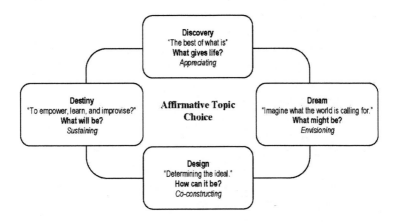

The AI 4-D cycle consists of the four phases (or stages) *Discovery, Dream, Design, and Destiny*. AI is best known for this 4-D model:[28]

AI 4-D model is a cycle of activities that guide stakeholders of a group, community, or organization through four stages: *discovery*—finding out about moments of excellence, peak experiences, core values, strengths, and best practices; *dream*—envisioning the positive possibilities; *design*—creating the structure, processes, and relationships that will support the dream; and *destiny*—living, improvising, and learning from best of the past and the novelty of the future to support the design of the dream.

This model was originally designed to help organizational systems adopt AI as an approach for achieving their dreams. Using the AI 4-D Cycle, all stakeholders identify and describe "what gives life" to the organization; together they imagine and create the future of their organization with relationships of energy, vitality, and commitment. This process has been used in leading thousands of organizations and communities through dynamic change initiatives. Each of the 4-Ds represent a phase or series of activities that link to the Affirmative Topic Choice. These are topics identified in the Discovery phase that focus on the intended change.

The AI 4-D Cycle in Daily Living

In daily living, the AI 4-D Cycle is a way to implement and practice the AI principles. In essence, the four phases of the cycle can be described as:

1. **Discovery** offers everyone the opportunity to realize how much their world is comprised of the stories they are telling themselves and one another—change the stories, change the world. Inquire into what gives life and the meaningful relationships in your life? What are the most significant stories of your life? Where are things going well in your life? Where are you making a difference? This is an opportunity to experience and witness the principles in action. Discovery engages the six core principles.

   Change the question➠ change the story➠ change your life and your relationships.

2. **Dream** asks, "What world do we want to create? What best possible dream can we share together?" Take time to envision the best possible future. This is another opportunity to experience applying the principles. During the Dream phase you primarily focus on the Positive and Anticipatory Principles; but it calls upon the other principles.

3. **Design** then asks, "How shall we live?" Create the structure/dynamics of relationships that support the dream. This is an opportunity to design relationships around the principles as they relate to the organization, community, and family dream. Design calls you to practice primarily the Anticipatory and Poetic Principles.

4. **Destiny** says live the principles—stay awake, change, improvise, be open, and flexible, practice the principles in alignment with the design and the dream will emerge. Engage in supportive intrapersonal and interpersonal relationships.

The original AI 4-D Cycle has been slightly modified, as shown in **Figure 2,** to be used by anyone to work through intrapersonal or interpersonal challenges, achieve desired outcomes, expand awareness, and generate meaning in organizations, community, and family systems. To use the process within an interpersonal relationship, you simply change "I/my" to "we/our." How the cycle plays out will depend upon the application or what is often referred to as the *affirmative topic.* Take a moment and study the Relational 4-D Cycle. Ask yourself, "What might this mean to me as I see it right now?"

If you are planning, developing, or seeking to achieve personal or group goals, the Relational 4-D Cycle can be extremely helpful. This process provides a means for discovering your strengths and successes, imagining your life as you would like it to un-fold, creating a design for the dynamics of daily living that will support your dream(s), and developing actions and relationships that support success.

Figure 2: The Relational 4-D cycle supports achievement of desired outcomes.

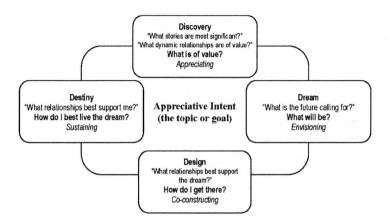

This cycle is a natural process for applying all of the AI principles we have introduced. Inquiry generates awareness around your best practices, strengths, values, opportunities, and dreams. Dialogue supports collaborative development of life plans which when lived generate the anticipated achievement or personal goal.

In the AI approach, the future of an organization is consciously co-constructed upon the organization's positive core. The concept of the positive core is central to the AI 4-D cycle. The positive core is made up of those strengths and opportunities that make up the best of an organization and its people. At the personal level, the positive core is made up of those life-giving intra- and interpersonal factors that define who you are when you are at your best. It is the stories within you that empower you and shine the light on your ability to engage in creating positive dynamic relationships.

The Principle of Awareness is fundamental to applying the Relational 4-D cycle in your development and the development of your relationships. You will recognize in the steps and exercises that follow in this chapter the practice of cycles of reflection and action in developing and expanding your awareness as you apply the Relational 4-D cycle in daily living.

Choosing Intentions

To apply the Relational 4-D Cycle in planning for daily living, begin by developing an awareness of your intentions (or goals) and how they impact your relationships. Frame your intentions in the affirmative and relational context (e.g., "I want to be on time because it shows respect for others" rather than "I want to stop being late because it irritates others"). You will have the opportunity to put the Principle of Awareness to practice here clarifying and exploring the variety of intentions you have for yourself. No one achieves his or her intentions in isolation and your actions toward your intentions will entail other people. As you write down each intention, be aware of the relational aspects.

❑ Major Life Intentions: Create a list of your major life intentions (attending to how they have been influenced by your relationships). They might be such things as creating and living a balanced life, losing weight or starting a business. In your journal, write these at the top of a new page in big bold letters. For example, you might write: "I will live a life that balances my work, family, and personal time". For each intention write how it will have a positive impact on your relationships.

❑ Daily Intentions: Begin your day with daily intentions in mind, especially ones related to your Major Life Intention. How do you want to relate? What do you want to do? Under the Major Life Intention listed in your journal, write, "Today I will . . ." Finish the sentence with one or more specific actions that you want to take today that will move you toward your Major Life Intention. We suggest making daily action-goals aggressive but obtainable. To continue our example, your daily action-intention journal entries might read: "Leave the office at 5:00 PM. Take a walk with my family after dinner and discuss the events of the day. Spend 15 minutes of uninterrupted time reviewing and working on my journal."

❑ Situational Intentions: Under your daily action-intentions, list several situations that you are likely to encounter today in which you would like things to change. For example, you might want a relationship at work to improve. Consider how your actions might support improvement and create a list of those things that you can do. Under the situation, list your expectation for what you would like to have happen? What will your actions be in that situation or in that relationship? How would you like it to be? You to be?

Situation—A co-worker asks for help on a big project and it is the end of the day.
Situational Goal—Explain that I have made plans for the evening, and offer to support her tomorrow.

Situation—A particular student in class continues to do poorly and be disruptive.
Situational Goal—Find a way to have the student play a significant and needed role in the class in order to bring him or her into the community.

Situation—My husband asks me to be home on time for dinner.
Situational Goal—Plan my exit. Schedule my last meeting so I am done working when the last appointment is done. I will have my briefcase packed up and ready to go before my last meeting so I can walk my clients out to their car and hop in mine.

Situation—The day ends and I am too tired to exercise or work in my journal.
Situational Intention—I start the kid's bedtime ritual fifteen minutes earlier and leave the extra time for myself.

❑ Observation Intentions: Observe others and develop the ability to understand them. Often this means asking them what they mean by statements or asking about assumptions. It may result in helping them discover clarity. This will do two things. First, it will develop your capacity for empathy. The better you are able to understand others the easier it is to act with appreciative intent. Second, watching how others cope with their situations and talking with them can help you learn ways to achieve your best intentions.

One last application of the Principle of Awareness before we move onto Discovery: reflect on your intentions. What do you notice about them? Where did these intentions come from; who or what has helped shape them? Who will be involved in your ability to achieve them? How has naming your intentions, purpose, or dreams influenced or affected you? What thoughts and feelings does this generate? Often when people begin to make explicit their intentions and purpose they realize it is not clear; they've never thought about them before. Just this minimal awareness can be valuable. If you don't know what your intentions are, then sit with the question. Being aware of our intentions, purpose, and dreams provides guidelines and a foundation for our actions in our relationships.

Discovery

The next round of reflection and action is to inquire into how you are already achieving your goal(s) or acting in ways that support achievement? What strengths do you have to support your success or achievement, what relationships do you already have that support this goal, and what are your dreams, wishes, and desires for achieving your goal(s)? This type of positive inquiry can also serve as a time of reflection into the best of your past and the ways it can be explored with an appreciative eye towards the future. If there were times of great struggle, stress, or pain in your life, inquire into the value of those times. What did you learn? What strengths and relationships enabled you to cope or triumph? What and whom do you have now in your life that you would not have if it were not for those experiences? (Put the Poetic Principle to work!) In this phase, you begin to discover your positive core. You can answer these questions in a journal; however, it is a more powerful activity if you do these exercises with your DR partner. Having a partner interested enough to ask questions helps you develop deeper awareness of who you are when you are at your best. The collaborative learning experience is much more likely to generate full awareness and greater learning.

Sometimes people find it difficult to identify their strengths. We are typically over-qualified in naming our weaknesses and much less savvy about those things at which we are naturally good. If you find this to be true, be sure to take one of the strengths-finder surveys on the Internet (listed in the next set of activities). Then reflect on how these strengths have played out in your life: where have they shown up? Or, work with your DR partner to help you discover your strengths. Being aware of your positive core will enable you to be a more valuable partner in any relationship.

When you engage in this discovery process with another, all of the Principles will be at play. This is another opportunity to practice them. As you talk with one another you will generate new meaning not only for yourself about yourself, but also from the other person about you. These changes will occur as you are speaking together. The questions you ask and the language you use will influence the changes. Pay attention to the nature of the dialogue even as you are engaged in it.

Practice the Discovery Phase

❑ Discover Your Strengths: To discover your strengths, reflect on your life, experiences, and relationships. When have you felt the most alive? What brings you the greatest joy? When do you feel that you are at your best for the least amount of effort? What relationships are positively engaging, energizing, and productive? You may want to have this conversation with family members, friends, and co-workers or even your boss. By asking others these questions, you will be able to see yourself from different perspectives and have richer conversation, learning, and exploration related to your strengths. Invite a shared conversation with someone else gathering feedback with regards to how others see your strengths and how you best use them. (Reciprocate with feedback for them about their strengths, providing they want to hear them.) Reflect on the feedback you receive. How does it compare with your personal assessment? How has each interchange with another influenced the relationship?

❑ Take a Strength Assessment: Martin Seligman's website on Authentic Happiness offers a free assessment that you can take on-line with results immediately available. Log on to www.authentichappiness.com and follow the link to the strengths assessment. You can also take the Strengthsfinder assessment at www.strengthsfinder.com. This one, however, requires a pass code, which can be obtained by purchasing the book, *Now Discover Your Strengths* by Don Clifton.

❑ Discover the Strengths of Others: If you have not done the exercise *Rediscovering Important Relationships,* first suggested in Chapter 2 in The Poetic Principle, do it now. Make sure you discover the strengths in everyone who plays an important role in your life. (As noted above, these relationships are highly influential in who you are now.) Then, in a journal entry, explore how you can make room for this person to use those strengths (to create better family living, to support the organization's mission, etc.). If you work with this person, reflect on whether the person's position allows his or her strengths to be maximized. If not, consider how things might change. If yes, make sure he or she has the leeway to maximize those strengths.

❑ Discovery Related to Intentions: Choose any one of your major, daily, or situational intentions and inquire into your current best practices related to it or how you are already succeeding at this goal. For example, if your goal is to live a balanced life, reflect on how you are currently doing that. Recall a period of time when you did an exceptional job of making time for work, family, friends, and yourself. Explore what was of value about you and those around you that made it work so well. How did others support your ability to do this?

❑ Find Your Sweet Spot: Your strengths are very important; however, they is more to the story. There is a diverse range of "assets" that enable you to add value to any situation. Besides your top strengths, it is important to be able to articulate your key experiences, skills, passions, thinking strategies, purpose, and values. Paul Hilt, calls this identification process "deep discovery". [29]

Deep discovery has two parts. First is the identification of content for each type of asset. Second is the identification of how all of your assets interconnect. To start make a list and consider using a visual display of information (such as a mind map). The intersection of these connections is your "sweet spot"—or positive core. When you have discovered your sweet spot, you will have a solid foundation upon which to build your most preferred future.

Again, reflect on this experience:

Q. How has your awareness shifted as a result of your inquiry?

Q. How have these questions influenced your relationship with yourself and those in your various communities?

Q. Did you experience a shift in your perception as the questions were explored (the Principle of Simultaneity)?

Q. If you shared this experience with a DR partner, how did this process impact that relationship?

Dream

The *Dream* phase calls you to imagine your preferred future, to dream the dreams of what could be and to experience them as if they were happening right now. It's the big picture. Imagine you woke up tomorrow and your goal was reality.

- Q. What would it be like?
- Q. What would you be like?
- Q. What has changed in your relationships and in your way of relating?
- Q. How would you be maximizing your strengths?
- Q. Who would be there?
- Q. Where would you be?
- Q. What would you value about yourself and others?
- Q. What would you be doing?
- Q. How much would you be working?
- Q. What would your relationships be like?

The greater the detail in your imagined, most preferred future, the better! This vision should be bold, dramatic, and written in the present tense.

Taking the time to actually write down your vision is valuable; the greater the detail in your writing the better. Note that it is important that this dream be realistic yet bold–a stretch. For example if you are 50 years old, don't envision a future where you are 25. Instead, envision a future where you have the things you value about a 25-year old, such as vitality, youthful looks, health, and vigor.

Some people have a difficult time dreaming; they have spent a lifetime limiting themselves by what they think is not possible. Some have been taught to consider dreaming a waste of time. Dreaming, however, is an application of the Anticipatory Principle and as such is an important component of creating a desired future. Find at least one of the exercises below that inspires you and expand into it. Dream big. Big dreams have never been known to limit what's possible!

Practice the Dream Phase

❑ Life Dreams: What do you want for your life and your relationships? On separate pages of your journal write a list of things you would like to accomplish, things you would like to do, things you would like to learn, habits you would like to develop, things you would like to have, ways you would like to be, ways you want your relationships to be, and ways you would like to give back to the world. Make sure as you create these lists you consider home and family, work, leisure, community, the world, and yourself. This is a time to dream. There is no place here for "oh, that's ridiculous" or "that will never happen!" If it's a dream, put it down. No limits! You should have at least 20 items on your list by the time you are done.

Now go through the list and decide which of these you would like to have happen in ten years, five years, three years, and the next year. Put a star next to the items that are the biggest priorities for each year (keep the number small—probably less than four). Then take the time to fully imagine that at the end of a year, these four things have been accomplished. How does it feel? What is life like? What did you do to make these things happen? What role did others play? How did it come about?

❑ Daily Dreams: Life dreams are big. They take commitment, time, consistent effort and persistent action to make them happen. Daily dreams can be the stepping stones to support us in achieving our life dreams. At the beginning of each day, imagine that the day is over and the day was perfect. In order for you to arrive at that point tonight, what will have to happen today? Make sure you cover home, work, community, and any other relevant environments and relationships. What role did you and others play in making the day turn out the way you dreamed it would? How did your actions generate the dynamics that supported the dream?

❑ Situational Dreams: For any given situation we often have a very specific desire or dream for how we want it to play out. This is especially true for the really important events, for challenges, for crises, and for events that have some significant meaning for us. Take the time before these events to dream. If they turned out just like you would like them to, what would have to happen? Who would be involved? What role would you play? How would others act and respond? What kind of environment would there be? What would you have done in preparation for the event to support the vision? Be as bold, bright, and as detailed as you can.

And now, reflect upon the experience of dreaming and imagining your future.

Q. How did the experience affect you?

Q. What thoughts or feelings arose as you went through this process?

Q. If you shared the experience with a DR partner, what impact did sharing the vision have?

Q. Did you find yourself thinking about how to create some of your dreams even as you were talking about them?

Q. Did the process impact your actions with others?

Design

In order to make the dream a reality, the third phase, *design*, requires knowledge, innovation, honesty, creativity, and most important, other people. In this phase you look at ways of living and relating that will lead to the achievement of your vision. This phase addresses the question–what kind of actions and relationships will best support your dreams and wishes? This phase calls us to shift from an emphasis on intrapersonal relating to interpersonal relationships, which most likely calls for new ways of acting. You move from your strengths to considering the dynamics of the relationships that are involved in moving toward achieving your goals. You need to consider how the dynamics of your relationships move you in the direction of your dream—and how you influence the dreams of others.

A poignant example of this was experienced by a friend of ours. She struggles to maintain her commitment to working out. One day she was at the gym and observed a group of five women who were working out together. They chatted, laughed, completed their routine, weighed in together, then high-fived each other. Our friend overheard one of the women say, "I would never be able to keep this up like this without all of you!" The light bulb went on for our friend, "The reason I struggle so much is that I am trying to do this alone; how much easier it would be if I recognized the importance of my relationships!" In the design phase, you build in and value the dynamics of your relationships as they are related to your dream.

Create a design statement. It should be an inspiring statement of appreciative action that is grounded in the realities of what has worked in your past, and written in the present tense as if it is already happening, and it should recognize and call attention to dynamic relationships. This is an opportunity to practice the Anticipatory Principle and Positive Principle. Ask yourself if the statement:

1. Is bold,
2. Challenges you,
3. Articulates your highest hopes and vision (or that of a group),
4. Supports your goal (or the goals of the group),
5. Supports appreciative action, and
6. Takes into account dynamic relationships.

To a large extent, this is where the "rubber meets the road." If your dream is to be physically fit, you must be willing to have part of your design contain those elements of living that create fitness. Essential to the design phase is open and honest awareness or recognition of the key components needed to create the life-plan that when lived will lead to the dream.

This part of the process requires that you reflect on your best practices as they relate to your dream. It challenges you to be creative and bring clarity to your goal or dream. It may require research in order to fully appreciate all that goes into achieving your goal. It is also important to realize that to accomplish this goal others must be involved and active in supporting your accomplishment. No one accomplishes a dream alone. It may be creating new relationships or changing the dynamics in current relationships.

Practice the Design Phase

❑ Using Other People's Stories: If others have accomplished what you want to accomplish, find out how they succeeded. Interview them. Gather information from many people and use that information to help you create a "strategy and structure" that will support your dream. How were they supported by others? What dynamics contributed to their success?

❑ Looking for Structure: Remember, your present patterns of being will continue to give you what you have always gotten. If you are not currently working towards the dream, you must do something different if you expect to bring the dream into full existence. Many people continue with destructive habits not because those habits work, but simply because they are habits. Changing outcomes means changing actions. As has been mentioned, changing habitual actions requires commitment. New habits are formed in only 4-6 weeks; you have to make the effort to follow through for those 4-6 weeks. (After that you must still follow through, but it gets easier and easier as your new habit comes a way of being). You must design a living system, a pattern of action, or approach for changing your present situation so that you are in a position to move towards your dream.

For example, if your dream is to be a lawyer and right now you are a paralegal, part of your structural change will involve creating the opportunity to go to law school. Some people find it helpful to look at the obstacles presently in their lives and then create plans for moving beyond those obstacles. Other people know right off exactly what needs to happen to move forward. Either way, now is the time to plan it and do it.

❑ Using Your Strengths to Bring Out the Dream: Armed with a myriad of stories and a solid understanding of the kind of actions it will take for you to live your dream, it's now time to use your personal strengths to make sure the design statement will be readily initiated and followed. Create a bold statement about how you live and act that incorporates your personal strengths. We used an example of developing an exercise and healthy eating plan. If you value family and security, and your strengths include competitiveness, creativity, and humor, here is how you might integrate these to support your dream of a healthy living style.

Health for a lifetime is ensured in our family because we use creative and fun ways to eat well and exercise together, enabling us to enjoy carefree time with one another.

Write it in the present tense, use action verbs, and if possible, keep it to a single sentence. In order to reach your dream, what will you do? Who will support you? Who do you want to be around? Who do you want to learn from? Your design statement should be focused on the process of knowing "what" you should be doing to make your dream a reality. It states what you must do in the present to achieve your dream. The *design* phase needs your creative energies. The more specific you can be, the more powerful your design statement will be.

❏ <u>Your Role in the Plan in Action:</u> Take a look at your role now in living your personal statement. Put "legs" on this affirmation so that it will be able to move. Those legs will be metaphorically your legs. An important question: What are the specific ways you will actually live this design? For the above example, you might create the following list:

1. Every weekend we take time to plan our weekly meals. We compete with one another to find fun, exciting meals that everyone loves. We use the newspaper, Internet, friends, and health magazines to find new recipes and visuals for ways to prepare beautiful food.
2. We shop once for the week, buying the foods needed to create our meal plan, and we enjoy finding the freshest food possible. We make shopping fun by playing games and joking with one another.
3. We take turns working together to create the meals. Each week we partner with a different person and have contests to see who can create the best meals that look the prettiest.
4. Every day we find creative ways to laugh and play together and that always gives us at least 20 minutes of heart-healthy movement.

Now, of course, reflect on your experience of creating your design statement.

Q. What were your thoughts and feelings?
Q. How has your statement impacted you and your relationships?
Q. Do you find yourself moved toward action even as you are still engaged in the process?

For many, the creation of the design statement can be challenging. You may find it easy to make a statement, but it may take a bit more time figuring out how to make it bold or provocative. Often people put their design statements in the future tense—check yours. If it's in the future, change it to the present tense. The mind will begin working and planning around statements that are in the present tense as if they reflect reality, regardless of whether they do or not. This is part of the power of positive image.

Destiny/Delivery

Destiny is about living, living into and toward your dreams and goals. Living the design takes flexibility, improvisation, commitment, practice, risk-taking, stretching, and the willingness to stay open to possibility. This is really the opportunity to continuously put all the principles into practice. Stay aware of the opportunities for moving towards your dreams. Look for ways to build your dream through shared meaning-making with others in your life. Be aware of the questions you ask and the questions you are asked; are they moving you toward your goals? Continually adjust the images you hold before you, engage in dialogue with others that develop bold and bright images for shared goals or dreams. You will be continually creating and recreating your future even as you move into it. Reflect continuously, stay aware and open to changing, improvising, and creating new movements that will support success.

Practice the Destiny Phase

❑ <u>Partners and Collaborative Learning Groups:</u> If you have not done so yet, find a DR partner or collaborative learning group now! Your partner may be a spouse or roommate. It might be a colleague at work or a good friend. It might be a mentor or a coach. Make sure your partner or the members of the group are people with whom you can talk and whom you can call upon for ideas, suggestions, and insight. They should be people who you trust to have your best interests in mind and to whom you are willing to listen to when they give you feedback.

For example, if your goal is to focus on the strengths and good things about situations, you want a partner who will stop you when you begin to complain about something. This requires a special relationship and a willingness on your part to accept that this is not criticism; it is supporting your ability to move toward the appreciative paradigm. Developing new actions and new ways of knowing will be challenged by old ones. Be open to feedback. It's not about being "right"; it's about living into your intentions.

❑ Just Do It: Become aware of your "inner voices"; they are very loud, strong, and convincing. If you have ever tried to change a habit, you know one of the voices we are talking about. It's the one that tries to talk you out of your new plan of action and back into the old comfortable living pattern. It's the one that has all the excuses for why this new design is not going to work today or in this situation. If you have a plan and it's a good one, just do it; work it; ignore that inner voice. Then afterwards reflect on your new actions in ways that support your new structure or design...and eventually you will hear a different inner voice—one that supports your new actions.

For example, referring to our healthy living design, when it comes time to go to the gym to work out, that voice might say things like, "You don't have time this morning, you'll have to do it later" or "You deserve to relax, you've worked so hard all day, besides you'll probably hurt yourself if you go exercise when you are this tired." Stop! Just go to the gym. Afterwards, reflect on your success. Consciously become aware of the strength building in your body, your energy level, your clarity of thought, and how you feel about your accomplishment.

❑ Recycle the Cycle: Support yourself by routinely reflecting on your being and doing in the world. At least once a week write a journal entry that invites you to discover the peak moments of practicing the principles of AI that week. Re-experience what it was like living that way. What did you value about yourself? What did you value about others? What happened as a result of acting in ways that supported your dreams? Imagine what it would be like if you could live every day this way. What would that be like? Feel like? How would your relationships change as a result? As you imagine that new future, what role are you playing in bringing it about?

Close with three wishes you have that will make that vision real. Then reflect upon those wishes; what can you do to make those wishes come true (Principle of Awareness)? What kinds of dialogue (inner and outer) will support them (Constructionist Principle)? What kind of focus of attention (Poetic Principle)? What expectations will you hold for yourself and others (The Anticipatory Principle)? And, what bold images of living those wishes are you willing to hold, commit to a story, or put into a collage (The Positive Principle)? Know that as you do any or all of these actions, it will move you closer to those wishes (The Principle of Simultaneity).

Reflect on each of the exercises that you did:

Q. What was the impact on your relationships?

Q. How did the activity support your dreams? What worked?

Q. What actions resulted in movement towards your dream?

Q. What needs modifying or adjusting?

Q. What happens after you make those adjustments?

Q. If you are working with a DR partner or group, how did you support other group members' dreams and goals and how did they support yours?

The above descriptions show you how to apply the Principle of Awareness and the Relational 4-D Cycle at the broadest level— to support your ability to create the future of your dreams. It can also be used with any relationship you want to consciously impact, any project at work, any interaction with a family member or colleague. It can be used for conducting a job search, planning a vacation, changing family or relationship patterns, conducting a business meeting, planning investments, furthering your education, starting an exercise program, preparing for a presentation or customer meeting, achieving departmental goals, or writing a book. Remember, if you can imagine it, you can apply the 4-D Cycle to it. The two key factors are:

1. Become regularly and purposefully aware of your goal(s) or dreams.
2. Practice the six principles, beginning with the Principle of Awareness.

To use the Relational 4-D Cycle effectively for your personal development, you must become aware of your intentions and the related dynamics of relationships in your daily life. Then you can work to turn your wants into reality by using the Relational 4-D Cycle to apply the principles on a regular basis.

Let's take a look at some examples. Each of the commonly experienced cases below describes a situation followed first by a traditional problem solving (PS)/judging thought pattern. Then there is a shift to an appreciative perspective that includes an example of movement through the Relational 4-D Cycle.

<u>The Project Plan</u>
❑ You have a proposal to submit and this is a crucial customer. It could mean a promotion for you.

Emotional Reaction and Thoughts: I've got to make this the best possible proposal. I'll figure this thing out and put it all together. If I want it done well I will have to do it myself since this is really going to be my client. Besides no one would be as committed since they have nothing to gain from it directly.

Appreciative Intention: I wonder how we (the organization) can best land this client, which would be great for the company and I might get a promotion from it? How can this happen?

Discovery: I look into successful past proposals; ones for big clients that were important for the organization to land. I ask, "How were they created and written?" "Who was involved?" "What strengths did each person involved bring and why were they of value?" "How were these proposals put together, presented, and what made them successful?" "Why did the client say, 'yes'?"

In the discovery, I learned the best proposals were clear on what the client needed. The client was engaged in the proposal process so the needs were fully appreciated and understood.

Dream: I imagine all the most appropriate people involved in putting the proposal together, including the client. In the best possible vision, we know exactly what the clients needs and desired outcome is and we have the ability to deliver that to him with impeccable quality. The client realizes our sincerity and works with us to generate a proposal that is a win-win.

Design: I develop a relationship with my client that supports our deep awareness of their needs, and our team has all the right skills and strengths to present our ability to serve the client in such a way that the client can only say, "Yes!"

Destiny: Practicing the principles, the best possible team was created. The team engaged the client in dialogue aimed at truly understanding their needs. We worked together, drawing on one another's strengths to compose the proposal and connect to the client.

The Silent Complaining Colleague
❑   You have a colleague who never speaks up and won't give his opinion or ideas at meetings, but then always grumbles

about the decisions afterwards. When he does complain he has good reasons why. It is very irritating that he always waits until after a decision to make his thoughts heard.

Emotional Reactions and Thoughts: This guy is really irritating. If he's going to complain afterwards he ought to just speak up in the beginning or keep quiet. Why doesn't he just come out and disagree in the beginning?

Appreciative Intention: I wonder why he doesn't speak up. He has great insight. It's bad timing when he speaks up after the meeting is over. I'd like to support his ability to be heard during the meetings. How do I help him to consider providing his insights in the meetings?

Discovery: I ask him if he'd be willing to give his opinion at the meetings if he were asked for it. While I'm at it, I ask him what it would take for him to just speak up without having to be asked, before we make any final decisions. And, I tell him we would welcome and value his opinions.

Dream: I invite him into my vision of his presenting excellent insight and helpful suggestions during the meetings so we can save time.

Design: I offer to help create the space for him to speak up until he is comfortable creating that space for himself. What might this look or feel like for him?

Destiny: The next meeting before any decisions are made, I ask him if he has anything to add. How does he best continue to contribute and be part of our team in creating policies, programs, and budgets? He is genuinely thanked and appreciated for his contributions.

The Mischievous Little Girl

❑ Your daughter seems to be incorrigible. She's only six years old. The list the sitter makes of things she does that deserve punishment seems to get longer and longer each day. You keep having the same conversations and nothing helps. You feel worse. You already feel bad for not being there when she comes home from school and you hate the idea of having to scold her every day as you say goodbye to the sitter.

Emotional Reactions and Thoughts: Anger, guilt; what can I do to fix this kid? What am I doing wrong? I feel so guilty leaving this child home so long.

Appreciative Intention: I want a healthy relationship with my daughter and I want a daughter who behaves well.

Discovery: I ask the sitter to make a list of all the good behaviors that my daughter has shown during their time together. When I get home at night, this is what I focus on. I discover there are a lot of good behaviors. I ask her what allowed her to have such a good day.

Dream: I acknowledge my daughter and invite her to imagine being so well behaved all the time. To myself, I imagine the same. I see it. Then, *we* see it. What does it feel like?

Design: I realize that my daughter is capable of choosing good behavior. I also know that what I focus on will grow and expand. How can we create the ideal day of good behaviors?

Destiny: I decide to pay attention to her good behavior, to reward that, and to provide incentive for more of the same.

If we analyze what is happening in the above examples, we will discover that using the Relational 4-D cycle fundamentally changes our underlying perceptions and our connections with everyone around us. This is more than just bumper sticker wisdom or pretending to be happy when we are not. When we choose to change the way we look at things, the things we look at change. Our choices around our living and relating change. Inevitably our relationships change; sometimes a miracle happens—our relationships improve and have more depth, meaning, and joy. Sometimes a different miracle happens—we change our relationships altogether (i.e., no longer stay in relationship with someone) in order to have more joy, health, and meaning. Whatever happens, the change will unfold in accordance with our appreciative actions.

It is important to note that this approach is not a process designed to change others. The reality is, that because relationships are dynamic, when we change, we impact others. Living the six principles of AI is an active, life-valuing approach that changes what you experience in the world by changing the only thing you can change: your thoughts and actions. By applying the principles to our actions we come to change the way we know—not only one another, but also the dynamics of those relationships.

Challenging Situations

The appreciative paradigm is relevant to any experience. Applying AI to difficult experiences—divorce, loss of a job, rejection of an application, lost sales, illness, or any struggle—may be a challenge. However, when you use AI in these situations, it has the most amazing impact. Doors open and opportunities appear. When faced with challenges, an important first step in making sense of what has happened is to accept that the situation you are in just *is*. Passing judgment on it, wondering whether it could have been different, or if you should have done something different, does not change your present situation or provide a positive way forward. *The important thing to recognize is that what occurs now, in this moment, between you and those involved is what is significant.*

Appreciating this is paramount. It allows you to let go of your initial perceptions, assumptions, and beliefs about the meaning of this experience in your life, freeing you to reflect openly and consider options for actions. This is a great time to apply Mama's rule about Mack trucks (Stop, Look, Listen, and Act). Ask questions about the experience that are different from those you might ordinarily ask. Inquire in ways that allow you to make sense of the experience so that you can move forward.

You might ask (or at least be open to),

Q. What value can come from this?
Q. Where is the opportunity?

You can also ask,

Q. What can I learn from this?
Q. How will who I am and the relevant relationships be affected by how I interpret what has happened?
Q. Who do I want to be and how can I interpret this situation in a way that supports me and others involved?
Q. What relationships do I have that can help me in this situation?

You might also look at the dynamics that generated this situation: the patterns of behavior, language, and interactions that resulted in your difficult experience. The most important pattern to look at, of course, is your own. In your reflection, the objective is not to judge, but to learn and ask:

Q. I wonder how did this come about?
Q. How did the dynamics of our relating bring this about?
Q. What role did I play in creating this experience?
Q. How do I want to act in the future?

You may have arrived at a fork in the road. Sometimes the fork in the road is an opportunity to make a new start, to choose not to be in relationship with another person or to choose another career—for all the right reasons. Other times you come to a crisis with people and you can make different choices while continuing to be in relationship. In these cases it is imperative to engage in this process *with* the other(s), working to create new meaning in the relationship. You can support changing your frame by recalling times with one another when there was a positive outcome (good times with an ex-spouse, a time your application was accepted, a time when sales were great). Changing your questions changes your focus of attention and thus changes the relationship; the Poetic Principle at work.

Either way, you can use AI as a philosophy for discovering positive meaning and opportunity in any experience. Apply *discovery*:

Q. What made those times so good?
Q. What did you value about yourself?
Q. What do you value about others?

Really *discover* the details that went into creating the good experience. Discover and define the positive core. Then move into *dream*. How do you want similar future situations to be? Imagine the ideal relationship together. Imagine the perfect interview, imagine completing an application that anyone would accept, imagine the best sales call. Apply the Constructionist Principle and the Principle of Simultaneity in the process of discovery and dream.

From this point, you can move on to *design*. Create the plan which, when lived, will move you toward the dream. It is the bold image and understanding of what needs to be done in order for your dream to become real. Practice the Anticipatory and Positive Principles in order to act in ways that move you *positively* forward. All that remains is for you to act upon and sustain your design. This is *destiny*. This is also a phase for continuous learning, adapting, improvising, and growing. The Principle of Awareness, if practiced in cycles of reflection and action, will support the sustainability of your dreams.

In a Nutshell

The use of the 4-D cycle in achieving your personal and relational goals and dreams is a powerful tool. Using it in conjunction with the six principles will move you rapidly toward the appreciative paradigm, where appreciative actions flow naturally. Patience with yourself, support from others, and practice are the simple instructions.

Here is a final, complete example of applying the 4-D cycle to a significant personal challenge. It is one that we hear often times at home, in communities and office conversations.

Initial intention or goal: I want to stop sitting on my butt, go exercise daily, and lose 10 pounds. I also want to stop eating sweets and fatty foods!

You no doubt recognize the traditional deficit-based language. The goal is described in terms of what you want to lose and what you want to stop doing. The images planted in your mind are: 10 pounds, sitting on your butt, exercise (a positive image), and eating sweets and fatty foods. Remember, we move in the direction of the images we carry. First we must reframe our desires in affirmative goals.

Affirmative goal grounded in relationship: I want to look and feel healthy and have my clothes fit comfortably. I want to exercise four times a week. I want to create an exercise program that realistically works best for me. I want to feel satisfied eating healthy foods like green vegetables, fruits, and lean meat. This will allow me to live longer with the people I love, be more effective at work, and have a lot more fun with family and friends.

The images here are look and feel healthy: comfortable fitting clothes; exercise four times a week; satisfaction with healthy foods, green vegetables, fruits, and lean meat. Again, we are more likely to move in the direction of our strongest images. These images need to be positive, bold, provocative, and compelling.

Now we can move through the 4-D process based upon our Affirmative Goal.

The Discovery Phase

There is power in the questions and that is where to start:

❑ Recall times in your past when you looked and felt healthy and alive, times when your clothes fit the way you wanted and you had lots of energy. What was happening during that time period? How did you feel? What were you doing? What did you value about others and yourself in your life at that time? What and who supported you?

❑ Recall times in your past when you did a lot of exercise. It may not mean going to the gym, it simply means times when you walked or hiked regularly, or times when you danced and moved a lot. What and who supported you doing that activity on a regular basis? How did it feel? What thoughts helped you stay committed?

❑ Recall times when you ate well, just the way you intended. What were you eating and how? Who was there? What kinds of food satisfied you? What kinds of thoughts and feelings supported your healthy diet? What did you value about yourself during that time? About others?

❑ Imagine living your intentions. What would it be like? How would you feel and look? What are you doing to live this way?

The Dream Phase

Here is where you create a bold dream with the images of the future you desire. You imagine looking and feeling the way you intend to be, grounded by connecting it to the experiences you uncovered in discovery and expanded into the ideal. You envision delicious, healthy meals served beautifully and enjoyed with your family and friends. And you see all the ways that you get exercise every day, enjoying the company of others who share your goal, making sure your whole body is exercised. Imagine yourself having thoughts, beliefs, and relationships that support this dream. Then create a collage of your desired future. Cut out photos of healthy foods, friends and family, and of exercise routines that are fun, engaging, and good for you. Get a photo of yourself when you were at your ideal weight and add it to the collage. Put this collage on your refrigerator.

The Design Phase

This step is essential for achieving the dream; without it, your dream stays a dream. If you want to achieve your dream, you must structure your living habits so that the dream comes about in daily living. This will take some effort at first, because it will require new habits. In the design phase, you need to create a pattern of living that nets your desired results. Begin by crafting a statement that captures the essence of your dream. Create that statement in the present tense, as if the future state was already present.

> I live each day full of energy, sharing the nourishing meals with my family. My friends and I enjoy working out together and this supports my ability to maintain a routine. I find joy in feeling my body stretch and I grow stronger every day, which further energizes me. I am amazed at my effectiveness and efficiency resulting from living as I intend.

In the design phase, you will find it is time to change, to apply lessons learned from conversations with your DR partner and your experiences with the exercises found in Chapters 2 and 3. Be aware of old habits of action and how they influence you. The real test of design is whether or not you have the courage to live the change you want to see.

The Destiny Phase

In the Destiny phase, you live your possibility statement. This is where you generate the dynamics in your intra- and interpersonal relationships that will support living your dream. For instance, you might interview people who eat well and ask them what they do to maintain that habit. You can interview people who exercise regularly and ask them what habits sustain them and how other people support them. Then you choose those things they shared that fit with you and create a new living pattern. You pull together a group of friends who are also committed to exercising and make a pact that you can all support and fulfill. Here is an example of a new structure:

❑ Early to bed and early to rise. Allow time for exercise in the morning before the day gets going and gets too busy. Think through the day and envision times set aside for activity; see yourself doing those activities.

❑ Plan the week's meals. Shop for only those foods that need to be cooked based on the plan. Buy fresh, wholesome foods. Take the time to prepare meals so they look appetizing.

❑ Brush teeth after meals so that your taste buds know the meal is over; this will train new habits of enjoying meals that consist only of protein, vegetables, complex carbohydrates, and fruits.

❑ Find a small group of friends who can schedule routine exercise at the same time you can and make a commitment to one another (or hire a trainer). Keep each other honest.

❑ Plan a varied exercise routine. Plan the days, including when and where you will exercise. Find an exercise partner and go with that person. Keep each other focused and committed.

❑ Review each day and acknowledge every day that a new habit is being created.

❑ Develop a set of thoughts that can be used to counter old patterns. *I feel better when I work out. Eating well gives me so much more energy. Don't think; just go; follow the plan.*

❑ Reward yourself for a job well done!

In this chapter, you have read and experienced the power of combining the Principles with the 4-D Cycle as a way to develop appreciative action and unleash the power of AI in daily living. You may also have experienced a shift in how you are coming to understand who *you* are, you may be beginning to experience yourself as a relational-collective being rather than as an isolated individual. Keep in mind that, just as before, no brand new way of relating or finding meaning in the world comes about overnight. If at any point you find yourself stuck and not moving towards your dreams, recall that you are not moving in isolation—ever. Pay attention to the relationship dynamics relevant to your dreams. What needs to happen for the dynamics to change in ways that will support your dream? What principle will help shape the dynamics?

There is a Zen saying, *"After enlightenment, chop wood, carry water."* This reminds us that whenever we have an epiphany, a great insight, a big ah-ha, we must then carry on with our daily living, challenged to implement our new awareness moment by moment. The purpose of this chapter has been to support your ability to chop wood and carry water with appreciative intent! This is also the challenge facing your communities of practice and choice. Using AI to sustain positive culture transformation is the subject of the next chapter.

FOCUS BOX

In this chapter we have introduced the idea of practicing AI at the personal level to enhance joy and abundance in daily living. We introduced the term *you* to refer to the collective person that you are.

Using the AI 4-D Cycle is a tool for discovering your dream and designing plans-for-action that will support the achievement of personal and community intentions and dreams.

We end this chapter where we began with a handful of questions:

❑   What are your personal visions for your life?

❑   What are your highest goals for your relationships with others? Family? Friends? Colleagues? Strangers? Children?

❑   What images do you hold regarding how you want to act at work?

❑   What are your dreams for the environment?

❑   What are your plans for giving *forward* to the world?

If you take time to *dream*, you will *discover* that *destiny* is yours to *design*.

Chapter 5

Sustaining
Positive Change

"We are confronted by insurmountable opportunities!"
~Pogo~

Appreciative Inquiry (AI) as a cultural transformation initiates profound insights for those who suddenly experience a new way of being in and making sense of the world. This way of being is best described by our friend, Jane Magruder Watkins, who says AI is "a habit of mind, heart, and imagination that searches for the success, the life-giving force rather than disaster and despair."[30] Sustaining that cultural transformation is a matter of supporting each community member's ability to *chop wood and carry water*. As we have suggested, this requires practicing the six principles and applying the Relational 4-D cycle in daily living. Learning to ask appreciative questions is also part of that process.

Inquiry is one of the most essential concepts in unleashing the power of AI in daily living and working. Recall the brief exercise in Chapter 2 to clarify the Principle of Simultaneity. We invited you to experience the difference between the impact of a problem-solving question and that of an appreciative question. To confirm the power of this comparison try the following exercise several times today or tomorrow:

❑ Consciously ask problem-solving questions with people and observe their reactions and responses. Problem-solving questions entail asking about what is wrong and what is not working in an effort to uncover what needs to be fixed. Notice what happens to the dynamics of the relationships; notice their responses, and the tone of the communication.

❑ Then consciously change to appreciative questions. Appreciative questions seek to uncover what is working, what is going well, what is of value in a situation, and what might be of value. Again, notice what happens to the dynamics of the relationships. Notice their responses, the energy level, and the direction of the conversation.

In each case below, become aware of the difference between the questions in the problem-solving (PS) example and those in the Appreciative Inquiry (AI) example. Notice how the PS questions will affect the relationship of those involved. What images and feelings do they generate? In what direction do they lead the conversation and the relationship? Do they elevate and inspire the relationship? Then explore the same questions with regards to the AI questions.

With Yourself

❏ PS: Why didn't I get more accomplished today? How will I get this done if I don't take it home? I am so tired, but I guess I need to bring the report home with me so that I can finish it. It's got to get done and there's no other way I'll be ready for the meeting at 10 AM.

❏ AI: I need to get this report finished by tomorrow and today is gone! I'm tired now. How can I be the most effective and efficient in knocking this thing out by 10 AM tomorrow? Let's see how much I've already done and what it will take to finish it. Hmm, I think I need a good night's sleep to refresh me. Getting here early will probably be enough.

With Your Partner/Spouse

❏ PS: I'm not happy. You're always tired and I'm tired of just watching TV. Why don't we ever do anything?

❏ AI: You know, we used to do more things together and I really loved those times; I miss them. Remember when we ... What would it take to start doing some of those things again?

With Your Children

❏ PS: Why aren't you on time? You've got to stop getting in so late at night after curfew. Perhaps grounding you for a week is what you need!

❏ AI: I really need you to be in by curfew. We have good reasons for wanting you home by that time. Not to mention that I worry when you don't make it in. Sometimes you manage to get here on time. What is it about those times that enable you to get home on time? How can we make sure that happens every time? I want to know you are safe. How can you make sure that I don't worry if you are running late?

With Colleagues
- ❏ PS: These missed deadlines are a real problem for the department. Why are you late? If you can't do the work, we can give it to someone who can.
- ❏ AI: Do you agree that when we get our projects accomplished efficiently and on time that we are in better position to achieve our goals? What do you need to help you make sure your work on the project is completed on time?

What did you discover as you experienced the differences between these questions? When you compared the PS and AI questions, did you see a clear difference in the dynamics of each relationship? Awareness of this difference is a key factor in understanding the power of AI in dynamic relationships; it is the guide that influences the development of the unconditional positive question.

Beginning the Process

The process of asking appreciative questions itself begins with a question: where are you and the community headed? For instance:

Q. What kind of relationships are you seeking to create?
Q. What needs to be achieved?
Q. What is the community looking to accomplish?
Q. What goals do you have?

Changing the way you inquire will change the dynamics in any interaction and hence the outcome. Asking these questions in an open dialogue with those involved will support a shared vision and shared understanding as to how you might move forward together in ways that meet everyone's needs.

Once you have a shared vision, continue to inquire. Recall from the fundamental Principle of Simultaneity that the questions you ask will instantly impact your relationships and the meanings generated in your conversation. You will either move toward what you want or away from it. The implication of this principle is that it is essential to inquire in ways that support the manifestation of your shared vision.

There are many possible options for inquiry: questions that generate ideas or best practices, questions that seek clarity and understanding, questions to solicit personal strengths, questions that look for value or search for times when something is working well or when someone or something is at its best. Identifying such questions often means suspending your actions long enough to inquire. It may mean looking for the opportunity or the means to bring out the best. It may even mean asking, "What is of value in this terrible thing that happened?"

Here are some examples of appreciative questions that you might ask on any given day:

The Self-Examined Life
❑   What is it that works well in my life? Who or what helps make it that way?
❑   What was the high point experience of the day and who helped make it a high point?
❑   What is of value in my life? What do I value about myself? About my family? About those that I work with and for?
❑   Where was I truly aware in my relationships today and what was the impact?
❑   What opportunities were present today and which ones did I take advantage of? Where were there missed opportunities that I could tap next time?
❑   What can I learn from today's experiences? And, what learning/insights can I take into tomorrow's experiences?

The Aware Partner/Spouse
❑   How can we do this differently so that we both feel good about it?
❑   What are the things that I love about him or her?
❑   What are her strengths and abilities and how do they support our family/relationship?
❑   How can we best communicate together?

❑ When are we our best as a couple?
❑ How do we bring out the best in each other? How might we do this even under stress?

The Aware Parent
❑ What did my son do well today?
❑ What is my daughter really good at? What are her strengths?
❑ Last week you kept your room absolutely spotless and I was so impressed. What was it about last week that made the difference in your ability to do that?
❑ Wow! Look at that paper, you got 85 correct! Good job. What do you think enabled you to get so many correct?
❑ What am I most proud of about the way my son or daughter is growing and developing?
❑ What was it about our relationship today that made it so good, open, and expressive?

The Aware Colleague
❑ I wonder how Sally is doing today. Perhaps she could use some help.
❑ What strengths does Ben bring to the team? What is the best use of his talents?
❑ You certainly think differently than I do about this. Tell me more about why you see it this way.
❑ This job is always such a struggle for me. I wonder if I am using my strengths to my best advantage. How might I succeed more easily?
❑ We met a huge challenge. What did we do as a team that enabled us to succeed?
❑ How can we work together in truly collaborative ways?

In asking and answering these questions, you will not only tap into those moments, special events, experiences, and full stories of the best, but you and those around you will also influence your perceptions and the immediate "next moment" in your lives. Your reactions, responses, and focus of attention are elevated by such questions, providing the energy, creativity, and inspiration to move forward.

In accordance with the AI Principles, *words create our world through shared understanding of language and interaction.* The moment questions are asked, appreciative dialogue takes us into a world that is full of positive emotions, language possibilities, strengths, motivation, purpose, and openness. Those questions move us towards our shared vision and dreams. Those engaged in such a dialogue have greater access to higher order thinking and creativity, greater capacity for health and improved relationships, and greater capacity for achieving organizational goals.

The asking of appreciative questions by an organization's senior leadership has a powerful effect, yet it is only the beginning for organizations that want to sustain positive changes in culture. Since organizations are simply a dynamic community of people with a shared purpose, the final ingredient in sustaining the positive change that unleashes the power of AI in the daily relations among employees is the people themselves.

Organizations and communities committed to the appreciative paradigm owe it to themselves to create collaborative learning groups that will support this transformation. Each collaborative learning group member can support other members on their journey towards appreciative action by working together daily. Imagine the potential for those organizations that move towards such a community.

FOCUS BOX

Sustaining positive change in our relationships and communities results from transforming the nature of our individual and collaborative inquiry.

We end this chapter with these key inquiry concepts:

❑ Develop a sense of wonder and curiosity.

❑ Use collaborative inquiry to discover a shared vision for where you want to go and what you want to create together.

❑ Be curious about what you and others are already doing that support that vision.

❑ Look for individual and community strengths and ask how they can be used to further your dreams.

❑ Ask questions that will generate images and information that move the community in the direction of the shared vision.

❑ Inquire into the ways you are succeeding.

❑ Expect everyone to have something of value.

Chapter 6

Beginning
The Journey

*"What we do accumulates;
the future is the result of what we do right now."*
~Pema Chodron~

This book is about living and relating from the stance of the appreciative paradigm. It is about making sense of the world as a dynamic system where relating in appreciative ways increases joy and abundance for all our relationships—families, communities, and organizations. It is about enhancing awareness through cycles of reflection and action. And, it is about making our work lives and home relationships more powerful. Recognizing that everything is integrally related and dynamic provides the foundation for suggesting that our relationships be governed by the six principles previously discussed. Practicing and applying these principles will unleash the power of Appreciative Inquiry (AI) in your life. Recognizing that inquiry is one of the most essential concepts in unleashing the power of AI in daily living and working is essential to this process.

We encourage you to make this a collaborative learning process. It is best if your Dynamic Relationships partner or group has read this book and is also seeking to develop the appreciative paradigm and appreciative actions as a way of relating. The purpose of this relationship with a collaborative learning partner or group is to encourage constructive accountability and to bring together thinking partners. Constructive accountability is a pattern of ongoing relational processes and actions that becomes possible during activities of cooperation, collaboration, strength enhancement, sensemaking, and contributions in everyday living.[31]

Remember, we are integrally connected to those in our lives and ultimately the way we understand is through our conversations, reflections, and actions. As David Cooperrider notes in his Foreword comments, "It is in the depth of our connections and conversations with others that we change ourselves and our relationships one conversation at a time." It is in relationship that we create opportunities for change that cannot exist when on our own. It is in relationship that our perceptions are altered. We must be aware that our perceptions heavily influence our actions. Having another person or group that shares your desire to change the way you relate in the world and is open to reflecting and learning with you is precious. The kinds of conversations, insights, and recurring stories that you share with one another will generate knowledge and understanding as well as encouragement and reinforcement. Invariably, you will move forward further and faster if you work collaboratively.

Choosing a Partner

The person or group you choose for a partner has significance in your journey towards the appreciative paradigm. When choosing partner(s), mutual respect and trust are essential. Accessibility and connection are important. You need to feel comfortable in being open, honest, and vulnerable with your partner or with everyone in a group. Share your journeys with one another. Ask learner-oriented questions of one another.[32] Share your insights, thoughts, and feelings. Practice creating appreciative questions and provide honest feedback. Have the openness and courage to challenge one another, question one another's assumptions, and practice the six principles. We guarantee you will discover, learn, and generate more insight and develop fuller awareness and greater skill in applying the principles if you are working with others.

If you have significant relationships with others who are not interested in applying the six principles in daily living, that is okay. If they show concern, reassure them that they do not have to change. The truth is, as you change, your relationships will change; this is the nature of dynamic relationships. Typically it is a pleasant change. If those in your life are threatened by your empowerment and growing ability to take responsibility for generating positive actions and relationships, understand the implications for the dynamics in those relationships and how their actions will influence your efforts. Appreciate that those who are threatened may be afraid. We recommend compassion but we also recommend setting boundaries that allow you to continue your own journey. If you do have such individuals in your life, we strongly encourage you to have a DR partner. If there is strong pressure for you to remain in a static relationship, without support, your efforts to live with appreciative actions are likely to meet resistance. Remember, relationships are dynamic; you are influenced by everyone around you. Most people will be pleased with the changes simply because they uplift and enhance your relationships.

In this final chapter, we want to emphasize the key concepts related to both the *appreciative paradigm* and *dynamic relationships*:

- You are an integral part of a dynamic whole. Your words and actions matter; the words and actions of others impact you.
- Words create images and images create the doorway into our future. Hold the most positive images by asking the most positive questions. They are compelling.
- There are always many options; the possibilities available for your words and actions are many. Make choices that generate exceptional relationships. Practicing the six principles will support you.
- Nothing is static. Everything is dynamic and fluid. It's not about you; it's not about the other. It is about the intersection of the two—*the relationship*—which can change in a heartbeat. Change your questions, change your actions, change your relationships, and change your world.
- Stay awake and live the paradox—continually step back to see your role practicing cycles of reflection (be the drop of water) and action (be the river).

The activities and exercises within the chapters of the book are there to support understanding of these concepts. Fully appreciating them requires trying the exercises to see how and where they fit and practicing them in your daily life to see what difference they make. When you practiced these exercises along the way, you probably experienced varying degrees of excitement in witnessing the six principles in action. In addition, you probably experienced both success and frustration in applying the principles in daily living. You may have experienced awe at the possibilities; you may have experienced fear of the responsibility. We hope you experienced the power of living AI.

At times, we—the authors—still find ourselves caught up in "ain't it awful" conversations or identifying the weaknesses in a system. Once we become aware of what we are doing we shake our heads at ourselves and wonder if we will ever get there. We must then remind one another that living into the appreciative paradigm is a journey, a continual moving toward a life of positive intent through the practice of AI—and that we are human. Only then can we release the self-criticism that holds us back from continuing on our journey. We encourage you to provide the same sort of support for one another and the same compassion for yourself.

The questions and exercises found throughout the book, as well as additional exercises, are available in a workbook, which is available on-line from the website www.dynamic-relationships.com. We emphasize as strongly as possible the notion that transforming your paradigm requires not only an awareness of the dynamics of your relationships, but also a commitment to practice the six principles on a daily basis. The Principle of Awareness is fundamental and key to change. For most of us, this means learning new ways of asking questions; for all of us it means committing to appreciative reflection and action. With commitment and daily practice, you will begin to develop new ways of knowing and understanding the very nature of your relationships that will ultimately allow you to live the six principles of AI effortlessly.

Writing this book has certainly been a collaborative learning process and we invite you to join this collaboration. We have been helped immensely along our journey by those ahead of us. If we share our ideas, insights, and stories with one another, we will learn more and discover better and simpler ways of effecting positive, inclusive change in the world. As we mentioned at the outset, we consider ourselves continuous learners on this journey, perhaps a half-step ahead of you or a half-mile behind. We want to hear your questions and comments as well as your thoughts, suggestions, and ideas for additional exercises and activities. We would also like to learn any insight you have for ways to unleash the power of AI in our lives and in our organizations. We invite you to visit and join the on-line collaborative learning community at www.dynamic-relationships.com. *There are many possible worlds out there. The probability that any one of them comes into being depends upon the dynamics of our relationships. What kind of world shall we live into?*

References

Adams, M. (2004).*Change Your Questions, Change Your Life*. San Francisco, CA: Berrett-Koehler Publishers.

Anderson, H. (1997). *Conversation, Language, and Possibilities: A Postmodern Approach to Therapy*. New York, NY: BasicBooks.

Cameron, K., Dutton, J., & Quinn, R. (2003). *Positive Organizational Scholarship*. San Francisco, CA: Berrett-Koehler Publishers.

Cameron, K. S., & Caza, A. (2004). Contributions to the Discipline of Positive Organizational Scholarship. *American Behavioral Scientists*, Kim Cameron and Arran Caza, Eds., 47, 731-739.

Clifton, D., & Nelson, P. (1992). *Soar with Your Strengths*. New York City, NY: Dell Publishing.

Clifton, D., & Buckingham, M. (2001). *Now Discover Your Strengths*. New York, NY: The Free Press.

Cooperrider, D., & Srivastva, S. (1987). Appreciative Inquiry in Organizational Life, *Research in Organization Change and Development*, W.P.R. Woodman. Greenwich, CT, JAI Press. 1: 129-169.

Cooperrider, D., & Whitney, D. (1999). *Collaborating for Change: Appreciative Inquiry*. San Francisco, CA: Berrett-Koehler Publishers.

Cooperrider, D. (1999). Positive Image, Positive Action: The Affirmative Basis of Organizing. *Appreciative Management and Leadership*, Cleveland, OH: Lakeshore Communications, Inc, pp. 91-125.

Cooperrider, D., Whitney, D., & Stavros, J. (2003). *Appreciative Inquiry Handbook: The First in a Series of AI Workbooks for Leaders of Change*. Cleveland, OH: Lakeshore Communications, Inc.

Cooperrider, D., & Avital, M. (2004). *Advances in Appreciative Inquiry: Constructive Discourse and Human Organization*. New York, NY: Elsevier Publishing.

Covey, S. (2004). *The 8ᵗʰ Habit.* New York, NY: The Free Press.

Fredrickson, B. (1998). What Good Are Positive Emotions. *Review of General Psychology,* 2, 300-319.

Frederickson, B. (2001). The Broaden-and-Build Theory of Positive Emotions. *American Psychologist,* 56, 218-226.

Fry, R., Barrett, F., Seiling, J., & Whitney, D. (2002). *Appreciative Inquiry and Organizational Transformation: Reports from the Field.* Quorum Books.

Gergen, K. (1994). *Realities and Relationships: Soundings in Social Constructionism.* Thousand Oaks, CA: Sage Publications.

Gergen, K. (1999). *An Invitation to Social Construction.* Thousand Oaks, CA: Sage Publications.

Gergen, K., & Gergen, M. (2004). *Social Constructionism: Entering a Dialogue.* Taos, NM: Taos Institute Publications.

Goleman, D. (1995). *Emotional Intelligence,* New York, NY: Bantam Dell Publishing Group.

Goleman, D., Boyatzis, R., & McKee, A. (2002). *Primal Leadership: Learning to Lead with Emotional Intelligence.* Boston, MA: Harvard Business Press.

Hammond, S. (1998). *The Thin Book of Appreciative Inquiry.* Bend, OR: Thin Book Publishing Company.

Kelm, J. (Expected Publication Fall 2005). Tentative Title: *Appreciative Living.*

Koestenbaum, P., & Block, P. (2001). *Freedom and Accountability at Work: Applying Philosophic Insight to the Real World.* San Francisco: Jossey-Bass/Pfeiffer.

Kuhn, T. (1962). *The Structure of Scientific Revolutions*. Chicago: University of Chicago Press.

Ludema, J., Whitney, D., Mohr, B., & Griffin, T. (2003). *The Appreciative Inquiry Summit*. San Francisco, CA: Berrett-Koehler Publishers.

McNamee, S., & Gergen, K. (1999). *Relational Responsibility: Resources for Sustainable Dialogue*. Thousand Oaks, CA: Sage Publications.

Paddock, S. (2004). *Appreciative Inquiry in the Catholic Church*. Bend, OR: Thin Book Publishing Company.

Palmer, P. (1998). *The Courage to Teach*. San Francisco, CA: Jossey-Bass.

Schiller, M., Holland, B., & Riley, D. (2001). *Appreciative Leaders: In the Eye of the Beholder*. Chagrin Falls, OH: Taos Institute Publications.

Seiling, J. (1997). *The Membership Organization: Achieving Top Performance through the New Workplace Community*. Palo Alto, CA: Davies-Black, an imprint of Consulting Psychologists Press.

Seiling, J. (2005). Unpublished dissertation on Moving from Individual to Constructive Accountability. University of Tilburg, The Netherlands.

Seligman, M. (1998). *Learned Optimism*. New York, NY: Simon and Schuster.

Seligman, M. (2002). *The Optimistic Child*. New York, NY: The Free Press.

Seligman, M. (2002). *Authentic Happiness*. New York, NY: The Free Press.

Senge, P. (1990). *The Fifth Discipline: The Art and Practice of the Learning Organization*. New York, NY: Random House.

Senge, P., Kleiner, A., Roberts, C., Ross, R., & Smith, B. (1994). *The Fifth Discipline Fieldbook*. New York, NY: Currency/Doubleday.

Stavros, J., Cooperrider, D., & Kelley, L. (2003). Strategic Inquiry with Appreciative Intent: Inspiration to SOAR. *Ai Practitioner*, London, England.

Thatchenkery, T. (2004). *Appreciative Sharing of Knowledge: Leveraging Knowledge Management for Strategic Change.* Chagrin Falls, OH: Taos Institute Publications.

Torres, C., & Weisenberger, C. (2005). *From Conflict to Collaboration.* Palo Alto, CA: LearningChange.

Watkins, J., & Mohr, B. (2001). *Appreciative Inquiry: Change at the Speed of Imagination.* San Francisco, CA: Jossey-Bass Pfeiffer.

Whitney, D., & Trosten-Bloom, A. (2003). *The Power of Appreciative Inquiry.* San Francisco, CA: Berrett-Koehler Publishers.

Zander, R., & Zander, B. (2000). *The Art of Possibility.* Boston, MA: Harvard Business School Press.

For most updated development in the field of Appreciative Inquiry visit http://appreciativeinquiry.cwru.edu. A website sponsored by Case Western Reserve University.

Endnotes

1. Gergen, K. *An Invitation to Social Constructionism*, 1999, pg. 101.

2. David Cooperrider created the original AI principles under the guidance of Suresh Srivasta during David's dissertation work. We have added a sixth principle: The Principle of Awareness.

3. Cooperrider D., et al. *The Appreciative Inquiry Handbook*, 2003, pg. 415.

4. Cameron, K., & Caza, A. "Contributions to the Discipline of Positive Organizational Scholarship", 2004, pg. 731.

5. Martin Seligman is the leading expert for the new movement of Positive Psychology, which focuses on mental health not mental illness. Several of the leading books he has authored in this field are in the Reference List.

6. Frederickson, B. "The Broaden-and-Build Theory of Positive Emotions", *American Psychologist,* 56, 2001, pg. 218-226.

7. *Using the autodesk civil 3D dynamic relationship-based environment.* Found at www.autodesk.com/civil3d, March 2005.

8. Dr. Marilee Adams has written two books in the field of question thinking. She proposes two paradigms of questioning, the judger and learner and how to best shift from the judger paradigm to the learner paradigm. For further reading: *Change Your Questions, Change Your Life*, 2004 and her first book, *The Art of the Question: A Guide to Short-Term Question-Centered Therapy*, 1998.

9. Palmer, Parker. *The Courage to Teach.* San Francisco, CA: Jossey-Bass Publishers, 1998 pg. 56.

10. Palmer, Parker, pg 56.

11. Anderson, H. *Conversation, Language and Possibilities: A Postmodern Approach to Therapy,* 1997, New York: Basic Books.

12. The AI 4-D Cycle (Discovery, Dream, Design, and Destiny) or AI 5-D (Definition is added) process. The most comprehensive source of information about AI is available at the AI Commons: http://ai.cwru.edu.

13. For a deeper dive into the latest theories and research across multiple disciplines that support the original AI Principles we recommend an upcoming book by Jacqueline Kelm, *Appreciative Living*, Publication Date Fall 2005.

14. Cooperrider, D., & Srivastva, S. "Appreciative Inquiry in Organizational Life", *Research in Organization Change and Development*, 1987. This is one of the first articles written on the core principles.

15. Ken and Mary Gergen are major contributors to the field of social construction. Please refer to the Reference List for a list of complete sources or visit the Taos Institute website at www.taosinstitute.net.

16. Cited from the Taos Institute Website at www.taosinstitute.net.

17. There is a whole body of literature that documents this phenomenon, alternatively called the "self-fulfilling prophecy" by teachers, doctors, and behavioral scientist that prove one's expectations shape another person's behavior.

18. In Greek Mythology, Galatea is a statue of a beautiful woman that was brought to life by the goddess of love, Aphrodite, because she was so desirable.

19. To learn more about the placebo effect and the power of positive imagery, these areas of research are detailed in Cooperrider's article "Positive Image, Positive Action: The Affirmative Basis of Organizing", 1999.

20. To read more and see video footage of Jane Elliott's story at www.pbs.org/wgbh/pages/frontline/shows/divided.

21. Cooperrider, D. "Positive Image Positive Action: The Affirmative Basis of Organizing." In *Appreciative Management and Leadership*, 1999.

22. Cooperrider, D. & Whitney, D. *Collaborating for Change: Appreciative Inquiry*, Berrett Koehler, 1999, pg. 27.

23. Daniel Goleman and Richard Boyatzis, are major contributors to the field of Emotional Intelligence that focus on how well we handle each other and ourselves. The five key principles are: Self-Awareness, Self-Regulation, Self-Motivation, Empathy, and Effective Relationships. Refer to the Reference List for key writings.

24. In the U.S. this is a colloquial phrase for being conscious. If one is "asleep", he or she acts as if they are not aware of what is happening around them. In order to make good choices then, they must "wake up."

25. This concept was originally conceived by Jane Seiling in her unpublished dissertation on "Moving from Individual to Constructive Accountability", University of Tilburg, The Netherlands.

26. Based on Jane Seiling's research a collective person integrates the subjective and objective learnings, experiences, thoughts, influences, interactions, hopes, and performances of multiple others—creating a unique collectivity of one.

27. Stavros J., Cooperrider D., & Kelley L. have created an approach to strategy that demonstrates how to do "Strategic Inquiry with Appreciative Intent" that provides the inspiration to SOAR! SOAR stands for identifying the organization's Strengths, Opportunities, Aspirations, and Results by organizational stakeholders.

28. Cooperrider D., et al. *The Appreciative Inquiry Handbook,* 2003, pg. 5.

29. For more information on "deep discovery" process contact Hilt & Associates, 30 Bridge Avenue, Berwyn, PA 19312, hilt.associates@verizon.net 610-246-4663.

30. Visit the website of Watkins & Kelley at www.appreciativeinquiry unlimited.com.

31. E-mail from Jane Seiling, June 3, 2005.

32. Marilee Adam's work best explains the essence of learner questions. For more information visit her website at www.CenterforInquiringLeadership.com.

About The Authors

Cheri Torres and **Jackie Stavros** have been collaborating for several years presenting seminars that combine the powerful approaches of Appreciative Inquiry and Experiential Learning. It has been their great joy and opportunity to co-author this book.

Cheri Torres, MBA, MA, and doctoral student in Collaborative Learning, is an educational consultant with MTC Associates, LLC. She has worked with hundreds of corporations, community organizations and schools to develop excellence through positive transformation. She co-designed and patented Mobile Team Challenge, an award winning, innovative, high performance portable low ropes course and has authored and co-authored numerous articles and books including *The Appreciative Facilitator: A Handbook for Facilitators and Teachers* and *From Conflict to Collaboration.* Cheri is an Associate Member of AI Consulting, LLC, is involved with Business as an Agent of World Benefit, a member of the Academy of Management, the Positive Change Corps (PCC), and the Association for Experiential Education (AEE). Email: cheri@mobileteamchallenge.com

Jackie Stavros, EDM, possesses eighteen years of strategic planning and organizational change experience. She is an Associate Professor at Lawrence Technological University

College of Management. She has done business in over a dozen countries in Asia, Europe, and North America. Jackie has authored several articles, "Strategic Inquiry with Appreciative Intent: Inspiration to SOAR!" and co-authored *The First Appreciative Inquiry Handbook: For Leaders of Change*. Jackie has spent the last 12 years incorporating Appreciative Inquiry (AI) methodologies into her teaching, training, and consulting work. She works with executives, managers, staff and line teams and an organization's stakeholders to collaboratively and creatively help them get organized and focused for profitable growth. Through AI coaching, she helps organizations identify and articulate their values, vision and mission statements, create strategy, and build collaborative teams for inspired action. Jackie is an Associate Member of Taos Institute and AI Consulting, LLC, a member of the Academy of Management, and a Board member of the Positive Change Corps (PCC). Jackie serves as a co-editor of the *Focus Books* Series for Taos Institute Publications. She has earned an Executive Doctorate of Management in *Capacity Building Using an Appreciative Approach: A Relational Process of Building Your Organization's Future* from Case Western Reserve University. Email: jstavros@comcast.net

Interested in Developing Dynamic Relationships throughout your organization or community group?

We offer the following services:
- ❑ Keynote and Conference Presentations
- ❑ Customized Workshops & Seminars
- ❑ Executive Retreats
- ❑ Coaching
- ❑ Customized workbooks for sustaining positive culture transformation

For quantity discounts on our book and to learn more about other services we offer, please visit our website at www.dynamic-relationships.com or contact either of us directly through the emails above.